# Forgotten People

# Forgotten People

*Catharine Brandt*

MOODY PRESS

CHICAGO

**Library of Congress Cataloging in Publication Data**

Brandt, Catharine.
    Forgotten people.

    Bibliography: p. 125.
    1. Aged—United States. 2. Helping behavior.
3. Aged—United States—Family relationships.
I. Title.
HQ1064.U5B7        301.43'5'0973        77-28968
ISBN 0-8024-2832-0

To my family,
who are indeed
reaching out to the elderly

# CONTENTS

# INTRODUCTION

All of us—children, young people, young married couples, middle-aged, the old themselves—have a stake in reaching out to the elderly. For all of us, if God grants the privilege, will one day be old.

In America today, 23 million people are over age sixty-five; many are more or less disabled, lonely, or have other needs. Frequently, those who have retired from their jobs harbor feelings of uselessness. Because many have few friends or relatives left to help them late in life, a feeling of isolation develops. Whatever their circumstances, the old have need of friends who will lift their spirits and minister to them in loving ways.

Yet in our youth-oriented society, little emphasis is placed on helping the old. Since their number is expected to double by the year 2000, we are certain to mingle more and more with the elderly.

Those who have never thought much about helping the aged can learn to lend a hand. This book gives practical suggestions for reaching out to relatives, neighbors, those in the church, and strangers. At the same time, as the elderly teach us to consider the last years of life, we will prepare for and understand our own old age.

A little attention will hearten the downcast; a little compassion will ease their uphill struggle; a little love and friendliness will brighten the darkest day.

Reaching out to the aged is a way to serve God, through the church or on our own, for God uses people in a thousand and one ways to deliver tangible evidence of His love and care to the elderly.

# 1

# HARDENING OF THE ATTITUDES

One hot August morning, after an hour in a nursing home, I took stock of my attitudes toward the elderly and found them wanting.

Two friends and I had volunteered to help with a Bible study that met once a week for a month. Pushing wheel-chair patients into the nursing home lounge, we settled them around a large table while other old ones tottered in.

The Bible hour started out like any might, but with a few differences. We sang from large-print hymnals (in several keys at once). When we talked about God's goodness, one serene-faced woman in a wheelchair thanked Him for good health (in a nursing home). Those with hearing and sight losses needed help finding the Scripture passage in their large-print Bibles.

As I plunged into the Bible study, silence spread over the group, except for one man who asked in a loud voice, "Is it time to eat?" Asking questions of them was like bouncing a ball against a garage door. No one caught the ball, so it bounced right back to me, while their attention wandered. *They're not thinking about the Bible story,* I thought. *No wonder they don't take part.*

What I did not know was that my attitude had caused me to misjudge those elderly ones. Some were shy, handicapped by strokes or by hearing and sight losses. Instead of them failing to respond, it was I who had failed to consider their limitations. I asked God to soften my attitude. The next week I did not expect them to discuss the Scripture passage.

When the month ended, the program superintendent asked if I would call on a few patients each week. At first I hesitated. Some were terminal cases. And I was not sure of any more success with calling than I had had with the Bible study. But I agreed to try.

On a one-to-one basis, I began to understand and love a number of old persons both in and out of nursing homes. I learned to look behind the wrinkles, the thinning hair, the crippled bodies and failing memories, and the crotchety complaints and demands to the person inside. I began to understand the heartbreak it must have been for them to leave behind a lifetime of dear, familiar patterns for unknown territory—old age.

Visiting one stroke victim, I soon ran out of things to say. "How are you?" I asked. "Can I do anything for you? Did you just have your hair done? It looks nice." Receiving no response except yes or no, I felt overwhelmed. What was left to say? Stopping at the nurses' station for advice, I found I had been taking a lot for granted.

"You go on talking," the nurse said. "She understands what you are saying, and she knows what she wants to answer, but some brain damage keeps her from speaking."

With that information, I redoubled my efforts in our one-sided conversation. One day I told her of an incident involving my granddaughter's black kitten. The woman's face crinkled into a smile. Then, speaking slowly, she said, "We—had—a—black dog—at home." That was a red-letter day for us both.

Changing our attitudes toward the elderly in nursing homes is one thing. What about parents and other relatives?

"My mother is driving us up the wall," a middle-aged man said. "She wants constant attention. When we visit her, all she does is complain and cry."

Another man said, "My wife's mother fell and broke her hip. She needs nursing care, but refuses to go to a nursing home. My wife and I both work, so there's little time for us to wait on her. She criticizes the helpers we line up for her and is very demanding."

The complaints and demands of the elderly may be caused by selfishness. On the other hand, these people may fear their loved ones no longer care about them.

When we are caught up in our own family affairs, it is easy to turn our backs on the aged. Our attitudes harden. Opening the Bible, we learn that God does not ignore the old. Instead, He promised long life as a reward for obedience (1 Kings 3:14). Another promise of God's blessing on longevity is, "Thou shalt come to thy grave in a full age, like as a shock of corn cometh in in his season" (Job 5:26).

That season arrives at different ages for different people. God has His own timetable for life. He has a purpose in allowing anyone to live sixty-five or eighty or one hundred years. The last ten years of life hold just as much purpose as the second, third, or fourth decades. Many need to be reminded of this truth late in life. So do quite a few younger ones who are, in our youth-oriented culture, conditioned to ignore those over sixty-five.

Misconceptions may prevent us from separating fact from fiction. "Old people can't be happy. Only the young can." "Old people are grouchy and complaining." "They live in the past and tell the same stories over and over."

A young woman with similar thoughts told her companion, "I never intend to be old: wheelchairs and no teeth or hair."

"Yeah," said the other, "but think of the alternative."

Besides spurning old people, the young woman was refusing to face her own old age. But refusing to be statistically old has nothing to do with reality. Unless death or the Lord's return intervenes, the future for us all, including teenagers, is old age. What will that future be like?

How to discard misconceptions about the elderly, and how to befriend those in our families, neighborhoods, and churches—as well as strangers—are questions that confront us all. At stake is not only the well-being of God's elderly children, but also our own old age. As we try to understand and learn from even one old person, we begin to prepare for our own future.

One way to understand is never to imagine that as the years go by all old people cease to be the same as they were when younger. Of course, some elderly ones are unlovable, untidy, complainers, or boring, just as are some people at any other age. But being old does not automatically change one into a cipher.

When asked whether she minded growing old, a woman in her seventies said, "I never think of myself as seventy or seventy-five but as a young adult. Of course, my body denies that," she continued. "I can't play tennis as I did when I was eighteen. A glance in the mirror shows my white hair and wrinkles. And I have experience and wisdom I lacked at twenty-five. But the part that is me isn't old."

She was saying what Victor Hugo wrote long ago: "Winter is on my head, but eternal spring is in my heart." That is why people of all ages can be friends with the elderly.

14

Another tendency we need to discard is the lumping together of the aged, whether inside or outside a nursing home, into one faceless group. Instead, they are individuals with diverse traits and needs—men and women for whom Christ died. And that is how we can reach out to them—one by one. If we reach far enough, we will find a needy heart.

A young woman admitted it took time for her to feel comfortable with old people. "They're so fragile," she said. "At first I was afraid that if I gave an old woman a squeeze I'd break one of her ribs." The aged are often fragile, but they are strong enough to sense love and concern.

Another woman relates how she helped her children develop right attitudes when their father, suffering from a stroke, spoke garbled words and walked with shuffling feet. "We won't act surprised," she told the children, "or pull away from Dad. We won't say or do anything that will cause him to feel belittled or think that we don't love and respect him as much as we did before the stroke."

A friend regrets that her stiff attitude as an adult kept her from hugging or kissing her father. "He lived with us for thirty years," she said, "and we thought a great deal of each other. But neither of us was demonstrative. Now that he's gone, I wish I had been." Of course, she had other thoughtful ways of showing her love.

When we face invisible barriers that keep us from expressing love to the elderly, we can ask God to help us overcome our reticence.

The elderly, with their needs, are a part of our daily lives: parents, grandparents, friends in church, neighbors, and strangers; old folks we touch and love; others that jolt and hurt us like a child's wagon bumping our shins. Still others are like freeway traffic that we scarcely notice as we whish by.

Young or middle-aged, men or women, up to our ears in work or with plenty of leisure time, we can change our attitudes and reach out. What those under sixty-five do to help parents and others stay active and independent as long as possible will doubtless improve their own future, as well as their attitudes.

That I would learn from the aged confined to a nursing home was a twist I had not expected. Yet as I observed them and other old ones, and as I listened to and encouraged them, my attitudes changed. I not only made new friends, but they also taught me much about patience, good-natured humor, gentleness, and serenity.

# 2

# NEGLECT OF THE ELDERLY

It is easy to mentally lump the elderly into one big group and neglect them. But when we see them as individuals with the same needs we all have, we will begin to notice them.

"As long as a person lives," writes Olga Knopf in *Successful Aging,* "he has feelings, desires, and needs that are no different from those he had when young. To be pushed aside . . . is just as painful at eighty as it is at twenty."[1]

Eighty-three-year-old Louise is one whose family is not pushing her aside. Active in literary groups, community projects, and her church, she lives in an apartment.

"For years," she says, "my goal has been to live my own life and be independent financially. I want my children and grandchildren to love me as a person, not just as a mother or grandmother." Louise admits she has worked hard to achieve her goal, and that she has been blessed with good health.

"This is a joyous period of my life," she says. "I don't cling to my family or demand attention. Yet we are often together. I feel secure."

Life can be joyous and secure for those over sixty-five who trust God and also have sufficient income, a measure of health, a sense of usefulness, and relatives who love them. Countless others, however, lack one or all of these securities, and are gripped by despair.

According to government statistics, nearly one-fourth of America's elderly are too poor to afford a decent place to live in or to buy nourishing food. Social security checks and old-age assistance are inadequate. They exist on incomes below the government-defined poverty level.

Frequently, the person over sixty-five is no longer part of a supporting group—at work, church, or even in a family unit.

Some old-age neglect can be solved only by better legislation. Pitching in to work for changes in state and national government is worthwhile, but outside the scope of this book. The emphasis here is on person-to-person help.

Authorities on aging declare that one form of neglect is failing to motivate older persons to help themselves as long as possible. We force them to give up the light work they could do and settle them into wheelchairs. We uproot them from their homes and plant them in "golden ghettos" (as someone has called retirement homes). By ignoring the aged, the church crowds them out of the pew, out of the church group, and into hours of television viewing and boredom.

As we read the Bible, we note how our Lord went straight to the neglected—the poor, the afflicted, and the despairing. Families, neighbors, and church members can all give of themselves in one-on-one help.

While on a visitation program for their inner-city church, two men walked around to the back of a house. They climbed the outside steps to the second floor and knocked.

"Come in," a man's voice called. In a poorly lighted room with worn-out furnishings, they found an elderly man, Charley, obviously in pain. The callers explained they were from the church a block away and asked if there was any way they could help him.

Charley told them his wife had left him and he had no relatives in town. Volunteers brought him "meals on wheels." "Tomorrow I go to the hospital to have surgery on my leg," he said, his eyes dark with fear.

One of the visitors made arrangements to drive Charley to the hospital. He stayed through the surgery and be-friended the sick man in other ways. After Charley's return home, one of the men brought him tapes of the pastor's Sunday morning sermons. All the while, the church prayed for the man's recovery.

Some months later Charley became a Christian, and shortly afterward his wife moved back to care for him.

Many old ones living alone or in nursing homes fear their children will forget them. In her book *You and Your Aging Parents,* Edith Stern states, "The fear of losing his children's love can become for an aging person, an all-pervading, almost constant terror."[2]

Theresa was a parent who feared that loss. She was placed in a nursing home in Minnesota while in her late eighties.

"My son lives in Connecticut," she said, "and he never comes to see me." Perhaps he had visited her, but in her confusion she had forgotten. Or the press of business, distance, and expense may have kept him away.

At first Theresa was alert enough to walk about and read the newspaper. But one day when I visited her she had had trouble breathing, so nurses had put her to bed and ad-ministered oxygen. Her hair was brushed back into a braid and her brown eyes were enormous. I held her hand, brown-spotted and gray-veined, and she would not let go.

19

We talked about God and whether she trusted the Saviour for eternal life.

"Oh, yes," she whispered. "I'm ready to go to Him." Then, so softly that I had to bend to hear, she added, "I wish my son would come."

One early morning God relieved that son of his responsibility; Theresa died in her sleep.

At times, those who mean to pay attention to the elderly may be unwise in their help. The daughter of a handsome woman in her eighties calls for her mother once a week to take her out for lunch and shopping. The woman is nearly blind and often spills her food.

"It's embarrassing for me," she told her neighbor. "I wish my daughter would visit me, but she says I deserve to eat out."

"I wish her daughter would visit her at home, too," the neighbor said. "She would be taking better care of her mother if she cleaned the stove and refrigerator and kitchen floor. They're a mess. But the girl is too busy to clean her mother's house."

Instead of taking her mother out for lunch and then pushing her out of heart and mind, the daughter might find someone to clean the house. Or she might find someone to live with her mother and care for her, thus postponing nursing-home care for a while.

The decision to place a parent in an institution is agonizing for most people. The problem is, of course, complex. What does one do when the children themselves are elderly, and both husband and wife must care for their aged parents? Or how about the sixty-eight-year-old man in Wisconsin whose wife is in a nursing home, while his ninety-year-old father lives in California? The father refuses to move to Wisconsin. The wife cannot be moved.

These are difficult decisions that require great insight and love.

How neglected the aged must feel when their adult children have little time to help them, or no room in their homes, or when they hustle parents off to a nursing home long before necessary. What a blow this neglect is to parents who remember how they fed and clothed and cared for their children when they were helpless and in need.

The fifth commandment in God's Book is not only a command, but also a promise. "Honor your father and your mother, that your days may be prolonged in the land which the LORD your God gives you" (Exodus 20:12, NASB).

A woman in a retirement home whose son is honoring her said, "I'm the only one here who receives regular calls from her family. My son lives in another state, but he calls me every Sunday, not just when I'm sick. He makes me feel I'm still part of the family. Some of the others here shed tears because their children never phone them."

College-age Sandra, a young person who shows interest in older people, said of her grandmother, "She's beautiful. Not face-lifted beauty, but the inner kind. She's wise and loving and likes to laugh. But she gets depressed sometimes just like I do, and she's willing to talk about it. I feel close to my grandma."

Judy, a young woman who pays attention to the elderly in her church, says, "I want to listen to Mrs. Anderson. Those lines on her face mark victory and achievement, as well as the aging process.

"She's fun to be with. Just by looking at her you can tell she has enjoyed her eighty-five years, that she is ready for her final exam. I want to hear what advice she has after being a Christian for so many years."

Of such elderly ones it can be said, "The older the fiddle, the sweeter the music."

Not all the elderly have wisdom and faith, or a sense of humor. Some are self-centered and long-winded, bitter and complaining. But all have need of compassion, understanding, and attention.

Any expenditure of time, money, or energy that enables the old to remain useful, to be active in the church, to live in their own homes, or to stay out of a nursing home a few more years or even months, will postpone their dependence. Such assistance may lift them out of despair and into hope.

# 3

# WHAT'S IT LIKE TO BE OLD?

Very few people under the age of sixty-five understand what it means to be old, a psychologist once said. His statement was based partly on the answers to a questionnaire given by a group of young married couples. Of the possible answers to the question: "What do you want most when you retire?" those checked most often were: (1) financial security; (2) freedom from responsibility.

When the same question was put to a representative group of men and women already retired, they checked two entirely different goals: (1) to be needed by others; (2) to feel self-esteem, to be somebody.

One of the most pressing concerns of the elderly, besides loneliness and lack of health or money, is loss of status or self-esteem. This is partly a fact of life in our society, and partly the result of failure to prepare for old age mentally and spiritually.

The church and individual Christians have a golden opportunity to talk to such old persons about God and to answer spiritual questions. For many older ones, there is not much time left. We can remind them, or explain for the first time, that in God's sight they are important, and that because of Christ's death on the cross they can be acceptable to God.

Those who have never thought much about tested and approved ways to help the aged will find a great deal of research has already been done by state and government conferences and by educators in the field of gerontology. (See Appendix and Bibliography.)

Knowledge also comes from what God says in His Word about the aged. "The hoary head is a crown of glory, if it be found in the way of righteousness" (Proverbs 16:31).

Another way to gain knowledge and experience is to make friends with older people and visit them regularly. They themselves can teach us how to be most helpful.

For example, it is better to give help the way the elderly want it, rather than by an extravagant gesture as we might think best. I learned that lesson one day when I visited an old woman in a wheelchair. She has poor eyesight and her hands shake from palsy. She was trying to mend a long run in a stocking, but the needle would not go where she wanted it to.

"Please turn on more light," she said.

"All the lights are on," I replied. "Why do you bother to mend that run? I'll buy you new stockings."

"Oh, no. I can't afford new stockings. After it's mended I can wear this one." She struggled again to put the needle in place.

"Let me mend the run," I said, taking the needle from her. In a few minutes I had finished it.

"Thank you," she said. "Your fingers are so quick. What shall I do now?"

Dismay hit me. I had taken a task from her that she wanted to do no matter how hard it was. "Do you have to do something?" I asked.

Peering up at me she said, "Have you ever seen my face when my hands aren't busy?"

"I'm sorry," I said. "Shall I find you another stocking to mend?"

"No. I guess I can't do it. Will you write a letter for me?" And that is what we did. I wrote while she dictated.

Thus, as we keep alert to what is already known about the elderly, as we search God's Word for direction, and as we make an elderly friend or two, we will begin to understand what it is like to be old, and how we can help those who are.

The aged often need help in the following areas.

## PHYSICAL HEALTH

Ill health can cause them to be cranky and uncooperative. Studies show that failure to exercise; poor nutrition; and lack of protein, minerals, and vitamins all contribute to depression and weakness. Often an old person struggles with impaired vision or hearing. The senses of smell and taste diminish, and it is easy to be forgetful.

"I can't eat this food; it tastes bad" may mean only that the old person's sense of taste is impaired.

On the bright side, many ailments formerly thought inevitable to old age can now be helped by medical care. It is important that the over-sixty-five person have regular care and advice from doctors.

Some old ones have difficulty speaking because of strokes. Shyness or stubbornness holds others back. It takes patience to draw them out.

## SPIRITUAL HEALTH

One authority on the problems of the aged says, "There are no capsule comments to compare with those in the Bible." Members of the older generation often have their favorite verses of Scripture. Why not help them look up new ones, a spiritual vitamin for each day?

Increased faith and trust in God plus knowing others care will help the aged overcome anxiety.

## FINANCES

Anything that holds down housing costs and health and tax expenses will provide some security. Some elderly may even be persuaded to work part time, within the limits of their strength, and so add to their income.

## FAMILY AND FRIENDS

Whatever we do to let the aged know they are loved and needed will help them. Just as they have given loving service to God and others in active days, so now in old age they can also serve. Help them find ways. Do not try to spare an elderly relative family troubles and tragedies. The old often surprise us with their courage in the face of disaster. They may even support us.

## INDEPENDENCE

An old person who has nothing to do soon becomes bored. It is then easy to be depressed and dependent.

The son of the famous painter Renoir recalled that his father refused to give up his independence. Renoir was seventy-five; his hands were twisted and deformed by arthritis, forcing him to hold the brush like a baseball bat. His son begged him to stop painting and visit a doctor.

But Renoir was unconcerned about finding a cure for his illness. Instead, he strove with all his willpower to keep painting. The greater his pain, the more he painted. Paralysis gradually took over. In those years before his death, when he refused to give up, Renoir painted some of his greatest works.

## SELF-APPROVAL

Help the old view themselves as worthwhile and useful. Activities that stimulate the brain and result in curiosity and reaching out to others will be a start in that direction.

What does it mean to be old? It means that one is near the end of life, not the beginning or the middle. It means one is frail, thistle-throated, with failing eyesight and hearing. Some doors are too heavy to push open. It takes longer to do things. More rest is needed, and responses are slow.

When I asked one woman in her eighties what it is like to be old, she smiled. "The pressures of middle age are gone," she said. "I no longer need to bake the best apple pie in the neighborhood. It's a time to weed out possessions, to weed out resentments, to forgive and ask forgiveness. To accept others the way they are. It's a time to endure pain and disability with good grace.

"It's the knowledge that each day I am nearer standing face to face with my Saviour."

The happiest old folks I know accept themselves as they are. They take a realistic view of wrinkles, cricks in the back, and other infirmities. They look on the positive side of any situation, and feel a responsibility to help others. They trust in the faithfulness of God to see them through the rest of their days.

Other old folks are not so content. What we do to help them reach out to others, retain a measure of self-reliance, perform a bit of useful work, and increase their faith in God will allow them to escape some of the woes of old age.

# 4

# THEY NEED LOVE

A minister once said the saddest word in the English language is *unloved*. A baby is born with the need to be loved, and none of us ever outgrows the need. Part of a poem by Donna Swanson dramatizes this.

How long has it been since someone touched me?
Twenty years?
Twenty years I've been a widow.
Respected.
Smiled at.
But never touched.
Never held close to another body.
Never held so close and warm that loneliness was
blotted out.
. . . .
They call me "Mom" or "Mother"
or "Grandma."
Never Minnie.
My mother called me Minnie.
And my friends.
Hank called me Minnie, too.
But they're gone.
And so is Minnie.
Only Grandma is here.
And, God! She's lonely![1]

Jesus told His followers, "This is My commandment, that you love one another, just as I have loved you" (John 15:12, NASB). Love one another in spite of old age, disablement, and infirmities? Love the old who are poor or of a different race? The unlovable?

If so, where do we start?

1. Go fortified by prayer and the Bible. For so simple a purpose as reading a psalm to an aged shut-in, read the psalm aloud at home first.

"We may not need the Bible in heaven," says David Allen Hubbard, president of Fuller Seminary, "but until then it has binding and absolute authority over what we believe and how we live. . . . God has spoken. We hear him. What more can we ask for? Just courage to proclaim and grace to obey."[2]

For those who have old ones close to them, prayer can provide patience, strength, and good humor. Any situation can be improved by these, plus a dollop of fun and laughter.

2. Be able to recommend the Lord Jesus Christ—what He is doing for us today and for eternity. Be able to point to Scripture verses that explain belief in the Saviour (e.g., Acts 4:12; 1 Corinthians 15:3-4).

3. Be sensitive to an old person's needs.

Mrs. Hanson, ninety-three, weighed less than her age. One morning unusual dizziness kept her from eating breakfast. Her daughter-in-law suggested she go back to bed. Then Irene called her husband. "Larry, Mother's color is bad and she's very weak. Why don't you come home?" In a few minutes Larry, over six feet tall and weighing 250 pounds, stood beside his mother's bed.

"How's my gal?" he asked heartily. Her whisper was too faint for him to hear, so he knelt down, put his arms around his mother's tiny, wasted body, and cradled her like a child.

"You're a great gal," he said cheerfully. Then he leaned his ear close to catch her reply.

"You're a great son." Before long her faint breathing stopped and she died, leaving a tender moment of two-way love for the big man to remember.

Old ones like Henry, living alone in his own four-room house since his wife's death, also need a touch of love. Henry's only son lives two thousand miles away in California. He wants his father to pull up stakes and move to California.

"Not me," Henry says. "Sure, I'm lonely, but my dog, Captain, keeps me company. I was born in Wisconsin and I'll die in Wisconsin."

Henry's stubbornness disturbs his son, and sharp words travel back and forth over the telephone. It is possible that Henry is better off in his own home in Wisconsin, but he needs his son's loving acceptance of his desire to stay. It is also likely that Henry would be happy in California, near his only son, but he will never know unless he tries it. Love on both sides would oil the machinery.

I want to praise a young man who showed his love for his ailing grandmother. She sat in a wheelchair in a nursing home. Paralyzed by a stroke, she spoke with difficulty.

With a burst of youthful energy, her grandson came and stood in the doorway of her room. He was handsome as any television ad model, with dark hair and eyes, and pink shirt and tie. His voice boomed out. "Hi, Grandma." He strode to her chair, put his arms around her, and kissed her heartily. "How are you?"

"Fine, Just—fine," she said with effort. Her hands lay heavy in her lap, but a warm glow spread across her face.

Old people have a longing for attention, for physical tenderness. They want to be loved; to be touched, hugged, and kissed just as they were when young. They like to feel important or useful to others. When such satisfactions are taken away, an old person may resort to illness, resentment, and surliness.

Love to the aged can also be expressed in a cherry smile, or in a gentle manner that overlooks spilled coffee, toothless grins, and absentmindedness. Those who are nearly blind or deaf respond to tenderness.

For the old folks far away, regular mail is a cherished expression of love. When a man expects his wife to write to his parents, she can suggest he write on special days, birthdays, and holidays. Then she can write regular, detailed letters of family activities. Grandparents prize and display pictures of grandchildren and their parents.

One more way to show love is to ask the elderly for their opinions or advice. Ask them. They may surprise us with the wisdom they have stored up during seventy or eighty years of living.

When we give ourselves in loving service to old people, we show them that someone cares about them. We also help them overcome one of the biggest problems of old age—loneliness.

There is a children's song that goes, "Love is something if you give it away/You end up having more."

# 5

# DOES ANYBODY HEAR?

As much as we may long to, it is impossible for one person to help all the old ones in town. But the simple act of listening carefully to one old person today, and then helping find an answer, may bring results. It may be the beginning of a changed outlook for your relative, your neighbor, or an old person in your church. Even the stranger on the bus. Listening shows that someone cares.

Of course, no one but God knows all the answers to the questions and doubts that arise to disturb the elderly. Still, using our God-given common sense and praying for empathy, we can help answer some questions an old person has.

**Has the church forgotten me? I've been absent six Sundays, and not a soul has called to find out if I am sick.**

"You feel cut off from your church?"

"Yes, I do. I've been a member for sixty years, and church on TV is not the same."

This forgotten person was a woman in her eighties, but she was expressing what many older church members are thinking. In previous years the woman had been active in her church, teaching a Sunday school class, heading the women's missionary circle, and entertaining young and old. Now the infirmities of old age kept her housebound.

A cheer committee and careful attention to homebound church members would help. It is important, though, to understand that many older people take offense more easily than when younger.

"I know I'm more sensitive in my late years," an elderly woman said. "I know I'm useless and can't do anything for my church. I can't even give as much money as formerly. But I don't want to be a nobody."

What homebound members can do that active ones sometimes neglect is to spend time praying. The church can give homebound older ones a list of prayer requests and needs, being sure to notify the one praying when answers come.

Special attention from the church will make the aged feel they are still a part of the congregation. Although their working and generous giving days are over, they still count.

**All my friends in the neighborhood have died or moved away. I don't know the newcomers. Nobody notices me.**

Help the bereft elderly one make a friendly move toward a newcomer. All of us need a close friend, one to whom we can confide and talk over problems. Perhaps the newcomers are longing to make friends, too.

**Why doesn't the Lord take me home? I'm a nuisance to everyone.**

That is a serious question for a person who has lived a long, useful life, and then is forced into a helpless, horizontal position.

"You feel there's nothing for you to do?"

"Yes. What can I do lying here?"

Pray? Witness? Listen to others?

A bedridden man said, "I try to be content. At least enough so my dear ones won't worry about me. It's waiting for death that's hard."

"O God, thou hast taught me from my youth: and hitherto have I declared thy wondrous works. Now also when I am old and greyheaded, O God, forsake me not; until I have shewed thy strength unto this generation, and thy power to every one that is to come" (Psalm 71:17-18).

**Why did they move me here? I don't want to be in a nursing home.**

Most of us dislike change, but a change can completely befuddle an old person. A few years ago the phone company in a rural area converted from the use of operators to the dial system. Some of the aged had to be taught to dial a number, and it was not easy for them to learn.

It takes time for an old person to adjust to a change of home. Failing to remember the room number can cause panic. When an old one complains about a necessary move, the answer must be, "You'll be at home after a while. You'll have good care here, and we'll visit you often."

**I wonder if my son and daughter-in-law are sincere when they say they want me to come live with them, or if they just consider it their duty.**

"You think they are just pretending they want you?"

"I don't want them taking charge of my affairs and telling me what to do."

34

This woman has been in charge of her own life a long time, and it will not be easy for her to change. She has been independent to the point of stubbornness in the past, so sometimes her children have left her alone. Now she doubts their sincerity. She needs to bridge the gap with love and trust, to ask for and accept her children's advice.

**I'm afraid I won't have enough money. Everything costs so much.**

Stella, a single woman, retired fifteen years ago. "I thought I was well-off," she says, "with my company pension, social security, the house my parents left me.

"Now I'm ready to go into a retirement home and I'm not sure my money will hold out. But I've put it in God's hands. He's provided for me in the past. I know He won't fail me now."

Financial insecurity is a gnawing worry to many old folks. A proverb tells us that it is not what we have that makes for security, but what we can do without. Old ones have fewer wants and can be frugal with their money. Still, fixed incomes offer no protection against inflation.

If there is a strong possibility of running out of funds, it is indeed a serious problem. Relatives should be informed, as well as the church. A younger man or woman with business acumen might offer to investigate possible sources of additional funds. There may be sources of income the old have overlooked.

**Do you think I will walk again?**

The man in the wheelchair asked the question with an anxious look on his face. I knew his legs had been useless for nearly four years, so I did not think he would walk again. But he wanted words of comfort.

"Oscar, how many walking years did God give you?"

"Over eighty," he said with a light in his eyes. "I used to walk all the way downtown and back. I used to walk clear out to Como Park and feed the monkeys in the zoo."

"You must have seen many interesting sights on your walks. God was preparing you and stocking your memory with pictures you can recall now while you can't walk."

"Yeah. Bridges built and buildings torn down. Trolley cars and fire engines pulled by charging horses." Oscar's eyes held a faraway look.

"Oscar, you've lived a lot of history," I said, "and you have stories to tell to others." He nodded, content.

### Why did I do this or that?

We do not know why. The fact remains the elderly woman did move in with her children, turning all her money over to them, and now she regrets that move. The old man did marry a young wife. That other man did lose his money in a risky business venture. She did dole out funds she could not spare to her alcoholic son.

Anyone has time to think of the past and regret mistakes when there is little of interest to fill the day. The old can ask God's forgiveness and make apologies to people if need be. Then we can help them forget the past. God gives us today, and the opportunity to rejoice in Him now.

### Why do I always forget?

Of course, no one who is mentally healthy forgets all the time. Poor circulation can cause the elderly to lose their thread of thought. Observe how young people also forget. "What did I go back for?" "Did I turn off the oven?" "I forgot what I was going to say."

Faulty memory is part of being littered with more facts, details, and decisions than we have taught our brains to handle. It is also a part of the wearing-out process of age. An older person should make notes and be doubly careful to check lights, stove, and locks.

### What is it like to die?

As followers of Christ, we have an obligation to speak of death to the aged. Advanced age can be a period of getting ready for death. Each day brings one closer to that day of meeting the Saviour and loved ones who have gone on before.

We cannot really tell an old person what it is like to die because we do not know. But we know all of life has been preparing us for the moment of physical death.

A couple drove to the home of the man's mother to take her out for dinner. When she did not answer their knock, they forced their way in. They found her sitting in a chair with her coat on and her purse in her lap. She was ready for the dinner date, but death had called for her first.

Her son said soberly, "She was ready for us, but she was just as ready for her appointment with God."

"Life is like an onion," goes a French proverb. "Peel it off one layer at a time, and sometimes you weep." The day is coming for the Christian when God will wipe away not only tears, but also wrinkles, arthritis, the knife-stab of pain, and loneliness.

In the meantime, listening is one of the loving acts anybody can do for the elderly.

# 6

# THROUGH A GLASS DARKLY

The farmer who delivered the eggs every Saturday morning counted out my change and picked up his egg crate. He was a big man; clean, though wearing a rumpled brown jacket, and a bit unsteady on his feet. Laughter lines creased his windburned face, but he was not smiling. His eyes held despair under the tufty black brows.

"How's your wife?" I asked. Last week he had told me she was ill.

"Poorly, ma'am. Poorly." He pushed back his white hair and wiped his forehead with the back of his hand. "Why, you know, she screams with pain when we have to move her in bed." He leaned against the doorframe with a look of bewilderment. "She's a good woman. Lived good all her life. Don't seem right she should be punished."

His words cried out for help. Although I tried to comfort him and explain my faith in God's love and care, I am afraid my help was inadequate. That was many years ago, and I, too, wanted to know the meaning of suffering.

Since then, someone introduced me to C. S. Lewis's book *The Problem of Pain*. By studying it and other books on the subject, plus the Bible, I have gained confidence to reach out to the elderly who are suffering. Not that I found answers to give, for as we search for answers we confront many mysteries. But we can offer comfort and hope.

The elderly often want to know, "Why do I suffer pain? If God really loved me, would He allow this?" If we want to reach out to those who suffer, it is important that we ourselves are sure of the sovereignty of God and His never failing love.

Why do people suffer? Some suffering might be termed punishment, the result of sin. We are too mulish or headstrong to obey God. "We can make our plans, but the final outcome is in God's hands" (Proverbs 16:1, TLB). And when our plans are contrary to God's intended "final outcome," we suffer.

We think we understand what causes some kinds of suffering. Unfaithful husbands and wives bring sorrow on themselves and their families. Unkind or selfish parents wound young children, causing them to suffer. Or we collide with God's world of law and order.

Usually, someone is hurt or killed when a serious accident occurs, whether the victims are children of God or not. Human error in the control tower causes a large jet to crash-land, killing hundreds. A car hits another head on. Three passengers with fractures and concussions are confined to the hospital for months.

Some physical pain and suffering are caused by lifelong grudges, hates, resentments, and guilt. Other pain comes from old bodies that are wearing out.

We understand such kinds of suffering to a certain extent. But we are baffled when we see some of the Lord's most faithful followers live their last years in unrelenting pain and adversity.

God's Word, from Genesis to Revelation, assures us of His supreme power and love. Yet alongside His power and love runs man's sin, the result of Adam's and Eve's disobedience in the Garden of Eden, the outgrowth of man's freedom of choice.

Millennia after that confrontation, we know from our own experience that "Man is born unto trouble, as the sparks fly upward" (Job 5:7). No one lives sixty or seventy years without experiencing many trials and afflictions.

The Bible teaches that though God does not *cause* pain and suffering, He *allows* it. Severely tested by Satan, Job lost everything. Yet God called him, "My servant Job." God allowed the testing, loss, and suffering, and used it all to strengthen Job's faith.

Three times the apostle Paul asked God to take away the thorn in his flesh. What was God's answer? "My grace is sufficient for thee: for my strength is made perfect in weakness" (2 Corinthians 12:9).

Our Lord Jesus prayed before the agony of the cross, "If it be possible, let this cup pass from me: nevertheless not as I will, but as thou wilt" (Matthew 26:39).

None of the above, including Christ, received easy-to-understand answers. Instead, as they bowed to the sovereignty of God, they were comforted by His love and presence.

When we try to comfort those in pain, some of us are like Job's friends. Those who have never experienced certain types of pain and suffering sometimes hop on a platform and expound on how the suffering one should react.

More effective than ready-mix answers is being on hand, assuring the afflicted ones we care, and helping them to faith in God's love. In his profound book on Job, *The Color of the Night,* Gerhard E. Frost says, "Job would have liked a light in his darkness, a ready answer to his terrifying questions. Instead he is given caring Presence."[1]

By God's grace I enjoy good health. I have never spent

months or even weeks in bed with constant pain, so I cannot fully understand that kind of suffering. But I can stand near those who suffer and let them know I care, reminding them of God's love, and reminding them that earth is not their permanent home.

Many times in the past I have begged God to relieve my mental or emotional despair, to release me from an unbearable situation, or to take away physical pain. Only when I struck the bottom of the valley and bowed to the sovereignty of God did I gain faith for the ordeal. "Lord, I don't like this. I don't see how I can endure it. But I accept it."

The Lord Jesus does not mete out endurance in one huge cornucopia for all the pain and suffering in the years to come. Moment by moment we are kept in His love. We receive grace for the present affliction, the *now*.

When we are called on to comfort and support the elderly in pain, we might encourage them to recall some previous tragedy or illness. The Jesus who gave grace to endure past trials will not fail them in the present one.

We can comfort those who are too ill to talk by a loving touch, a handclasp, or by just sitting beside them.

A minister whose jaw was broken in a car accident suffered intolerable pain. Later a man asked, "What did you do those days in the hospital when no drug helped?"

"Ah! I couldn't pray," he replied. "All I could do was put myself into the Saviour's hands. Over and over I called His name, 'Jesus! Jesus!' until such time as I could pray again."

Others might lack his strong faith. Faith often fails in great pain and illness. God may use us to strengthen their weak faith. What those tortured by pain need is not a recital of *our* past pains and illnesses, but the knowledge that someone is supporting them in prayer with loving concern.

They may be helped to acknowledge afresh the hand of God in all things, even pain and suffering.

" 'For I know the plans that I have for you,' declares the LORD, 'plans for welfare and not for calamity to give you a future and a hope' " (Jeremiah 29:11, NASB). Those plans are for here and the hereafter, and they are sure to include pain and suffering—to the strengthening of faith, that He may be glorified.

# 7

## ROOM IN THE HEART

"We can't leave Dad alone now that Mother's gone," Alicia told her husband. "But how in the world can we take him here? Jim needs his own room and privacy. The girls won't give up their room. I don't see how we can have him."

When George's eighty-three-year-old mother suffered a stroke, he moved her into a room with nursing care. She had lived previously in an attractive apartment in a retirement home. But George made her give up her apartment and pack away her belongings. "Now she'll be taken care of," he said, "and we won't have to worry."

As the date for her husband's retirement neared, Paula grew impatient with her mother's demands on her time. Because the older woman was ailing and had only a small income, Paula feared her mother would have to move in with them, upsetting their plans for travel.

Alicia, George, and Paula all had one trait in common. They were looking for a surefire, one-step method for taking care of their parents. But no foolproof, instantaneous method exists. Ways to discharge responsibilities toward parents are as varied as the parents and children themselves.

What makes the situation puzzling to many sons and daughters is that they have never been old. They cannot put themselves in an old one's place, or imagine what it is like.

43

"We assume," says David O. Moberg, sociologist, "that their needs are material only; if they have sufficient incomes to meet their basic needs of food, shelter, clothing, and possibly a meager allowance for medical expenses, then our responsibilities to them are fully met.

"Actually, their greatest unsatisfied needs relate to their psychological, social, and spiritual problems."[1]

They need to be loved by family, to be useful to others and right with God—heart needs.

Recently we have seen a change in how people care for elderly parents. Nursing homes sprang up like dandelions in the 1960s because we wanted a safe place where Mom and Dad could be taken care of until they died, and not outlive their assets. Even the old folks liked the ideas of security and of having things done for them.

In the intervening years, those concerned have had second thoughts. The bloom is off some nursing homes, caused in part by overcrowding; exposé articles; government investigations; and especially, rocketing costs. Some charge $1,000 or more per month.

We are beginning to understand what gerontologists have said all along. A nursing home is not necessarily the best place for an elderly parent. Nor is a comfortable room in a son's or daughter's home with nothing much to do always the right solution. Either may be the quickest route to an aged parent's decline.

Alternatives to moving in with adult children include hiring someone to live with the parent, part-time nursing care, day care, a foster home, or a retired persons' residence with a private room and central dining room. (See Appendix for services offered in many communities.)

Taking advantage of such help will mean less disruption in the lives of all concerned. Studies show that those who stay in their own homes are healthier and happier than those who give up and let a son or daughter take care of them. Drs. Doris G. and David J. Jonas emphasize in *Young Till We Die* that the elderly should remain in their own homes as long as possible.[2]

We ought to give credit to those who have enough spunk to want to stay in their own homes.

When living alone is no longer feasible, the parent, instead of abdicating all familiar surroundings, possessions, and independence, and moving to a nursing home, may be better off living for a time with a son or daughter.

Some adults, though, cannot for various reasons invite a parent to live with them. Some parents have sharp corners and prickly ways. So do some children. The older ones may rub their children the wrong way, as Beverly's father did. "He's seventy-five, going on eight," she told a neighbor, "and I'm ready to tear my hair out." It may not be wise for them to live together.

How to help elderly parents is a knotty problem, but one that cannot be avoided. A fundamental precept is to let parents know they are loved and respected, and that they have someone they can trust.

"Having someone to trust is very important," a friend of mine in her eighties says. "If children would just realize this and build up trust, it would mean much. I'm thankful every day because my daughter and son-in-law have proved over and over that I can trust them."

Besides building up trust, a son or daughter can give the warmth of companionship. I recall how after my husband's death my daughter-in-law said, "We don't ever want you to be alone on a holiday." Then she followed through on that remark.

Another opportunity to build trust may arise when it is

45

necessary to check on a parent's health. An apple-a-day approach to medical care is not enough. Make sure they understand good nutrition and visit their doctor regularly.

Find out what they can do—a balance between napping all afternoon and spading the garden. We need to take into account how long it takes for the old one's body to recover from extra effort. There may be an energy shortage. If Dad overworks one day, see that he rests more the next. Do not try to hurry old people, but encourage them to take their time.

Responsible health care for parents includes trying to prevent accidents around the house and protection against crimes, committed so often against the frail and preoccupied elderly.

How far one may go in insisting the parent receive adequate health care depends on the parent. Those who are self-sufficient will be in charge of their own health. But even they may need a warning: "Dad, why don't you knock it off for a while and take a nap?" When it is necessary to give advice on health, it can be done with loving-kindness.

Children can work to reverse the bad attitudes of parents who tend to feel sorry for themselves, or who withdraw from a place in society and the church. They might ask help from their parents.

A woman I know said, "The older I grow, the more I must lean on others for some help. It's not an easy adjustment. What makes it easier is when my children lean on me a bit and ask for advice, baby-sitting, recipes, or to borrow something I prize highly."

What causes many elderly persons to feel anxious, dissatisfied, and useless is the lack of a daily pattern of something worthwhile to do. To help parents keep their self-respect, Edith Stern, in *You and Your Aging Parents*, suggests

46

giving them things to do and think about. She writes, "Not 'How can I entertain Mom or Dad?' but 'What can I find for them to entertain themselves?' "[3]

It may take more time to get a parent organized to bake bread than to do the job yourself. The payoff will be the older one's satisfaction and contentment.

"I can be bored and hurting all over," one man says. "If I can put my hands on something worthwhile to do, I forget my ailments."

Many of the activities in chapter 10, "They Help Themselves," can be modified and practiced by less-active old folks.

Adult children will go a long way toward untangling the knot of what to do about aged parents if they show their love, make sure their parents trust them, and help parents feel useful.

Still another tangle arises because the child-parent situation is packed with emotion.

Sharp words from Paula's (the woman referred to earlier) mother helped Paula understand what was important to the older woman. Paula frequently answered her mother's complaints curtly. Underlying her ungracious replies was resentment that her mother's coming to live with them would alter their way of life.

One day her mother said, "Paula, you are in the driver's seat now. Some day you may know what it means to be lonely and sick and without money."

The words stabbed Paula. "Proud words are not easy to recall," Carl Sandburg once wrote, but Paula knew she must. She put her arms around her mother and asked her forgiveness.

Later Paula wrote to her brothers and sisters. Together they agreed to each send a monthly check to their mother.

The checks enabled her to stay in her own little home for the rest of her days. Knowing her children had room in their hearts for her changed her from a bitter, depressed woman to one with self-respect.

When a disabled parent does move in with a son or daughter, other family members should help make the decision. Brothers and sisters should be in on the planning and expense. A single son or daughter should not be expected to assume all care and expense. Each one in the family must be sensitive to the parent's needs, realizing that giving up his or her home means losing independence and place in the community.

Establish ground rules before the move. Consider and discuss how much the parent will contribute toward household expenses, and how much help, if any, will be expected from the parent. Expect as much self-help as possible, but never take advantage of the parent's availability or willingness to help. There must also be privacy for the parent—not just a folding bed in the living room.

My mother lived with us for twenty years before she died, visiting my brothers' and sister's homes at regular times of the year. Our family enjoyed many blessings from this arrangement. At the same time, there were pitfalls.

Now, with hindsight, I believe it would have been better if we had tried harder to help her live in her own place. At the time it seemed impossible, and we assured her we had room in both our homes and our hearts. She did, though, become dependent on others sooner than was necessary.

When three generations live together, we would like things to run smoothly. At the same time, we are unwilling to accept the truth that living together may produce an occasional explosion. Even though adult children appreciate their parents' love and care in the past, conflicts arise. Wrapped up in the love and appreciation are hidden resentments and guilt feelings caused by real or imagined past injustices. When the parent-child role is reversed, the parent, too, may feel resentment.

"Since Mother moved in with us," Avis complained to a neighbor, "it's just one more cause for a fight with the kids." What Avis failed to understand is that the antagonism of young teens is, in most cases, actually directed toward parents, not grandparents. Grandparents often provide a stabilizing influence in the home, as the following illustrate.

"My grandpa has lived at our house since I was a little kid," Bruce says. "He's almost blind. When I come home from football practice, I go up to his room and read the headlines and the sports to him. He waits for me to come."

Carol says, "My grandma likes TV. We watch programs together. She likes games too—Flinch and Scrabble and Rack-O. Our family plays games on Sunday afternoons."

Karen, who sewed her own clothes, took her yard goods and patterns to her grandmother's room for approval. Afterward she modeled the finished garment. Her grandmother's praise encouraged Karen. At the same time, being included in the girl's sewing projects bolstered the old woman's feeling of self-worth.

Such situations do not just spring up, as Carla discovered. One morning she dashed out the door, yanked her toddler to safety, and slapped him smartly on his little behind. His shrieks brought Carla's mother-in-law, who lived with them, to the door.

"Why is the baby crying?" she demanded.

Carla explained Timmy had disobeyed and played in the street. Her mother-in-law picked up the child and comforted him. "You ought to be ashamed," she told Carla.

49

Since this was not the first instance of friction between the two women, Carla later talked with her husband, trying to find out what was wrong. They thought they were the only ones who faced the problem of a parent with a negative attitude. After receiving counsel from their minister and reading books on old age, they realized that when parents live with their married children a clash of personalities often occurs. They learned that the older woman's critical outlook probably reflected her own feeling of insecurity, and they resolved to make her understand they loved her.

Now, when her mother-in-law is overly critical, Carla brushes it off with, "I don't think you really mean that, Mother." Then she tries to find something for the older woman to do. While Carla prepares dinner, she asks her mother-in-law to take charge of Timmy. "It's the time when I have end-of-the-day-itis," Carla says. She is quick to praise the older woman for her help, and a smoother relationship has developed.

A "cooked-out" mother might suggest the opposite and spend time with her child while the grandmother prepares the meal.

A grandparent living in a three-generation home might be asked to help with family devotions, reading the Bible and praying about a good relationship in the family. Private prayer on both sides will ease tensions. I once heard a minister say, "If you feel like shaking someone, the best place is in your prayers."

If a parent becomes incapacitated, incontinent, or in need of help in eating, then a nursing home may be the answer. Countless adult children cheerfully assume the responsibility for such care for disabled parents who lack funds. Others feel bitter resentment when money earmarked for a family vacation or college education for the children must be spent on a parent in a nursing home. Such tensions need to be resolved, perhaps with government help, so that the parent does not feel his children are waiting for him to die.

Not everyone is able to give a parent the care at home a friend of mine gives her one-hundred-year-old mother. Along with her great age, the woman also suffers many physical failures. My friend gives her mother tender nursing care, and often must be alert twenty-four hours a day. Some of us wonder how she does it. Wouldn't it be easier to place her mother in a good nursing home?

"She's my mother, and I love her, and this is my job right now," my friend said. "It may get to be too much for me, but now we sit and knit or sew together. Mother is still alert and interested in the news and baseball. We take advantage of nursing aid and help from relatives and friends."

She makes another point. "Before placing a parent in a nursing home, great care should be taken to prepare the aging one. It can be a shock. I'm just not ready to do that."

Some old ones may be too confused to understand the reason for the move. In strange surroundings they cannot think straight; they feel abandoned, that they have been dropped off to die. The family should visit often during the first weeks an elderly parent spends in a nursing home.

Easy, surefire solutions are not often found for the problems we have been talking about. "Life is hard/By the yard," a terse verse-writer suggests. "But by the inch/It's a cinch."

Perhaps not a cinch, but as we work at the tangled knots day by day, our responsibility to parents becomes a little easier and clearer. In the emotion-packed situation of children caring for parents, love and laughter play important roles. When there is room in the heart for an aged parent, things have a way of working out.

# 8

## "I WAS A STRANGER"

It is often easier to show interest in a stranger our own age (or even younger) than to reach out to one who is elderly. We sense a barrier between ourselves and the one we think of as old. One time I asked my son to tell me when he thought I had grown old.

"Mom," he said with a grin, "you were always somebody old to me."

Taking advice from the writer who said, "If you can't laugh at yourself, it's all over," I laughed.

Then I asked my son's teenage children who they thought were old people. "Dad and Mom," they replied promptly. We were joking about a well-known truth—old age is relative. No matter how old we are, someone is always older.

Even peppery ninety-six-year-old Nellie knew that. Her roommate in the nursing home had just died, and already she missed her.

"I hope you enjoy your new roommate," I said.

"Well, just so I don't get somebody old like the one who was looking at the room yesterday."

Besides the barrier that separates us from the one we consider old, there is also the distance between us and strangers. When the psalmist wrote, "I am a stranger in the earth" (Psalm 119:19), he spoke for all of us. If knowing we are all strangers on earth is not enough to make us reach out to those we do not know, our Lord's heart-touching discourse in Matthew 25:35 should rouse us to do so: "I was a stranger, and you invited me in" (NASB).

Strangers move into our town, neighborhood, or apartment complex; or into a mobile home park, high rise, or retirement center. We visit a nursing home, mental institution, or prison. Wherever we are—on the bus, shopping, in church—we see elderly strangers. And Christ's words echo in our thoughts. "Inasmuch as ye have done it unto one of the least of these my brethren, ye have done it unto me" (Matthew 25:40).

Mel and Helen left long time friends and relatives to move to a retirement home filled with strangers they had never seen before. When Helen's doctor ordered her not to do any heavy housework, they sold their house and furniture, keeping just enough to furnish a small apartment in the comfortable retirement center.

"For us it's the best solution," Mel says. "Our children are old folks themselves, and the grandkids have their own lives to live. With all the noise and dogs and babies, a Sunday afternoon visit is long enough for us. We like our peace and quiet.

"Moving into this retirement center meant we had to get acquainted with a lot of strangers." Then he adds with a chuckle, "Some of them are pretty old."

Helen, who spends half an hour each morning with a lonely widow down the hall, says, "She talks nonstop. All her aches, fears, and resentments. And she repeats herself."

It is annoying to listen to complaints and twice-told tales. Garrulous old ones are usually lonely or needing to relieve tension. Either way they need a listening ear. Sometimes we can stem the meaningless tide of words by asking a question.

"Where did you live as a child?"

"Won't you tell me about your wedding day?"

"Do you have any children? Grandchildren?"

"Has God done something special for you this past week?"

"Do you have a favorite Bible passage? May I read it to you?"

"Will you let me tell you what Jesus means to me?"

Helen tried several of those questions with her talkative neighbor. "Gradually," she says, "the woman turned from self-centeredness toward others and thinking about the present."

Mel spent the first two weeks in the home roaming up and down the halls and watching the clock until he realized he had better make new friends. "When you live in an age-segregated commune," he said, "you have to love your neighbors because the others are too far away."

Many who retire move to a warm climate and settle in a mobile home park, far from grandchildren and old friends, with strangers all around them. The Seeleys, for example, liked everything about their new mobile home. But just sitting in the sun was not enough for them. Formerly active members in their church up north, they wanted to be part of a Bible study group that would help them grow as Christians.

Dorothy said, "I inquired but found no such group in the park. The Lord impressed on me that we needed a Bible study in our park to stimulate thinking and help us get to know others. For some time I prayed that someone in the park would lead such a study. I talked to several who encouraged me but were not interested in starting a Bible study themselves."

*Well, I tried,* Dorothy thought. *That's the end of it.* But it wasn't. "My concern for such a group grew. Was God telling me to lead the Bible study? For two years I fought the idea. Finally, I told my husband I thought I would try."

Dorothy visited a local religious bookstore, bought a Bible dictionary, a commentary, and a Bible with four comparative versions. "I also depend a great deal on Henrietta Mears's *What the Bible Is All About,*" she said.

Then Dorothy began studying the book of Luke. Next she asked the manager for permission to hold the Bible study in the library. "I put a notice on the recreation hall bulletin board that I would be leading a Bible study the next Tuesday morning and anyone was welcome. Then I went home to pray and study, and waited the hour with uncertainty. Who was I to teach God's Word to those who would come?"

Six came for the first Bible study. "I really praised God," Dorothy says. "Now, three years later we have twenty to twenty-four. Besides Luke we have studied James, Genesis, and the Acts of the Apostles. Because of the turnover of residents in the park, we often have newcomers."

Soon after the Bible study started, one couple came to the Seeleys and said, "We have prayed for a Bible study group for some time. This is an answer to prayer."

Dorothy said, "The biggest plus for me was that I learned to depend on the Lord. I often went to the study group with trembling knees, but God saw me through. I have grown in my knowledge of the Bible and how it applies to my daily life."

Various ones have thanked Dorothy for leading the group, and for the way the Scripture has been explained and discussed. Onetime strangers, they have talked over each other's problems in the light of the Scripture studied, and have come to know and depend on one another.

One way to be available to help older strangers is to see individuals in any crowd and develop a sensitivity to their needs.

Fran did just that. She stood on the corner on Hennepin Avenue waiting for the bus. Busy shoppers halted for the lights while traffic whooshed by. When the lights changed, everyone surged across the street. Fran, watching the crowds, thought, *Dozens and dozens of people, but no two look alike or dress alike.*

Gradually her eyes focused on a bent old man, who was crossing the street with the others. A red plaid beret topped his white hair, and the collar of his black coat was turned up to ward off the wind.

"That's the second time he's gone across Hennepin," Fran said under her breath. At the other side the man turned and walked a few feet down the street. He shook his head, stopped, and looked around uncertainly while people bypassed him. Then he walked back to the intersection and crossed again to where Fran stood. She moved closer to him and smiled.

"Are you looking for some place?" she asked.

The man peered at her with cloudy eyes. "Yes," he said. "I'm going to meet my granddaughter at Dayton's. I thought this was the corner."

"Look," Fran said, "it's a block down the other way. I'll show you."

They started out and after a bit the man said, "I see it. Thought sure they'd moved the building. Thank you, miss." Then he winked at Fran and trudged off down the street.

Fran missed her bus, but she says, "I'm glad I didn't miss the old man's wink."

If it seems difficult to speak to a stranger, we can remember that all people, no matter what their nationality—whether young or old, rich or poor, energetic or sick—understand what one writer calls international language. A wink, a nod, a smile, a handshake, and perhaps the expression *OK* are all universally understood.

A smile can brighten the day for anyone—the one in front of the smile and the one behind it. It can leap across the barrier between us and a stranger.

# 9

# THEY'RE IN THE CHURCH PEW

A young minister received a call to a small, city church. After the first service his wife said, "They are practically all 'white-heads' in this church. Where are the young people?"

"Yes, there are quite a few old folks," he said. "And the church isn't doing much for them. I'd like to try." He organized three elective Sunday school classes. This brought young and old together. He also pulled the older ones into service on committees so the church would benefit not only from agitation and energy, but also from wisdom based on meditation and experience. He interested young people in visiting shut-ins and those hospitalized, and in transporting the infirm to meetings.

Gradually, a number of young married couples joined the church and helped reach out to the aged.

Churches spend time, money, and manpower meeting the needs of youth and adults: cradle roll, youth groups, and junior choir; young mothers' morning Bible study and couples' club. Such commendable programs are part of a lively church. Equally important is planning for the old.

When older ones come, do all but the pastor ignore them? When the elderly are absent, who makes a friendly phone or house call? Some aged ones may be too weak or frail to let the pastor know when illness strikes, or they do not want to bother him. They think they are not important enough. Like many younger ones, they deny the fact that old age is an important part of the life cycle.

And so, long before necessary, the old ones stay home and watch a televised sermon. While they lose the fellowship and communion of the saints, the church also loses their help. Under such circumstances, not many of us would feel important or useful. Yet every older Christian is a part of the Body of Christ. If elderly members hurt or have needs, the church has a mission to be concerned and reach out to them.

Is church work piling up or being undertaken by young people only, while those over sixty-five are sitting it out?

Before answering, try to imagine what it is like to be alone, unable to drive, with few relatives and friends left, and even fewer contacts in the church. Topping all that, many old persons lack money to buy new clothing every season. Some see this as a barrier to being accepted in their church.

Like Ezekiel of old, we need to sit where they sit for "seven days" (Ezekiel 3:15). All of us need others who love and care about us, and whom we love and care about in return. The aged especially need new friends to replace those who have died or moved away. Of course, no old person is without love when he has the Saviour. Still, the Lord Jesus has chosen to use His followers to provide human love and help for others.

One solution would be to refrain from segregating the elderly into "senior citizen" groups. Instead, pull them into all church activities as the young minister did in the opening illustration.

Those in charge of church affairs should tap the wisdom and potential usefulness of the old. Their patience and dependability equip them for such tasks as library work, office work, phone reassurance, publicity, calling on the sick, repairing choir robes, and compiling the church's history. They can teach knitting and other skills to young people.

Long time members know how the church is progressing, or perhaps falling down, and should be called on for advice.

Instead of racking our brains to think of programs *for* the old, we can draw them into existing activities that will bring them close to all ages. Feeling a part of their church will strengthen their self-reliance, which is so vital to the continuing health of the old.

Suburban church congregations, composed chiefly of young couples and their families, might search out the older people connected with their group, even if it means driving across town to pick them up. The church needs the old and the stability they give.

Many of the following ideas and methods that some churches have tried and found workable might, if modified, fit the needs of other congregations.

## PRAYER

When the sale of the building she lived in forced eighty-year-old Mrs. Wheaton to find another low-cost apartment in the neighborhood, the Tenth Avenue Community Church moved into action. For two months, privately and at regular meetings, they prayed that a vacant apartment close to the church would become available.

As families talked about Mrs. Wheaton's need and asked God's help, even little children prayed that she would not have to move out of the neighborhood. No one was surprised when she found the right place just before the deadline. Several men used their muscles and station wagons to help move her belongings.

"I'm glad I didn't have to move away." Her voice held an un-eightyish lilt. "My church means so much to me."

### CHEER COMMITTEE

In small churches, the cheer committee might be headed by a regular attender who will record absentees. Able-bodied old ones can visit them. Even shut-ins near a phone can be useful making calls.

Others in the church should alert the cheer committee when they know of one who needs help or a visit. The older person, too, needs to notify the pastor or the secretary when he or she is ill, goes to the hospital, or has a serious need.

In larger churches, where those present register each Sunday morning, an older person can help organize the list of those who need a friendly letter, phone call, or visit.

A variation of the cheer committee is a program Calvary Baptist Church, St. Paul, Minnesota, used to draw young and old together. Members who were willing to spend time on the program each supervised six or seven others. Quite a few over-sixty-fivers participated. The church membership was divided into groups with a mix of old and young, longtime members and newborn Christians, regular and irregular in attendance. The "caring chairman" kept a sharp lookout for absentees.

In times of stress or need, people could call their chairman for counsel. If warranted, the "caring chairman" relayed the need to the pastor. One chairman said, "It's easier for one person to watch over six or seven assigned people than for the entire church to be responsible for the whole congregation." The success of such a program depends on the amount of time the "caring chairman" puts into it.

Similarly in a small church, University Avenue Congregational, St. Paul, volunteers were asked to open their homes for an evening of fellowship. The host invited half a dozen assigned persons for coffee and dessert.

We entertained an elderly couple, a widow, and three school-age children in our home. While the children played games the adults talked. In the informal evening we all moved closer to one another, a relationship that continued for some time.

## ANNUAL SHUT-IN DAY

One church holds its Sunday school classes once a year in the homes of those too feeble or disabled to attend services. By prearrangement the class (children, youth, adults) goes to the invalid's home. The class visits briefly, sings, and recites Scripture; the teacher leads a short Bible study.

Someone with a camera may take a picture of the shut-in and the class, presenting a copy to the invalid.

A home department, where workers regularly visit shut-ins and teach a short Bible lesson, is the best answer.

## TELEPHONE REASSURANCE PROGRAM

What happened some years ago to a well-loved member of one church need not have occurred. The woman suffered a fatal stroke and lay alone in her apartment for several days before someone found her. She had no phone hookup with another member of the church.

The church might set up a program similar to one used by the police and other organizations. Each helper is responsible for two or three names. The one who is ill or alone calls the control person at a certain time each morning. If the sick one is likely to forget or be confused, then the control person makes the call. If there is no response after a call or two, someone goes to investigate.

## BOOK CLUB

One church has a book-reading club that draws all ages, including a number of over-sixty-fivers. A committee chooses a religious book for each month, buying enough copies for the group. Each one pays for a book, then reads it at home. The group meets one Sunday afternoon a month to discuss the book and apply it to church life.

Even those who read widely have profited by reading books they otherwise might not have chosen.

## CHURCH HANDYMAN

A notice in *Modern Maturity* states that many old people complain they cannot afford the high cost of household repairs. A retired handyman in the congregation might repair small appliances or other household items, perhaps on a reciprocal basis, receiving, for example, a loaf of homemade bread for repairing a lamp cord. A young couple might shovel snow in return for baby-sitting.

## PRACTICAL LECTURES

Lectures or films on good nutrition, appropriate exercise, and financial management, while helpful to the old, may also be of interest to the middle-aged, and even young couples. These not only have a stake in the future of the aged, but also need to accept their own future old age with confidence. The church might investigate and inform older members of community services—public library, transportation, group dining, home-delivered meals, home aides, and "senior citizen" meetings.

## CHURCH LIBRARY

The church library should be a resource center on problems and ways to help the elderly.

## VISITATION

Before his retirement as a full-time pastor, Clarence Anderson regularly rounded up some of the older members of his church for a calling afternoon. He dropped one of his helpers off to spend an hour or so at the home of a shut-in. The pastor stopped a moment to visit the invalid, prayed, and then drove on to the next shut-in. When all his helpers were delivered, he returned to pick up the first helper.

At other times he took a carful of junior choir members or Christmas carolers to sing for the shut-ins.

## TRANSPORTATION

Possibly the biggest need of many old people is getting about. Furnishing rides may well be the ministry that takes the most time and forethought. Many older ones no longer drive, and public transportation is not available or is too far away. For a young couple to sacrifice their time and desires in order to pick up one or two old ones for church services is truly reaching out.

The church might appoint one person to be responsible for matching rides and riders—not only for Sunday services, but also for trips to the doctor, dentist, hospital, and grocery store.

Ruth Clausen, an enterprising older woman, volunteered her hands and time to quilt with the elderly ladies of her circle.

"I had a reason," she said with a chuckle. "I made a patchwork quilt, but didn't know how to do the quilting. When I saw the beautiful work of the ladies' circle, I wanted them to do my quilt.

"They told me they had orders for two years ahead. That's when I volunteered to learn how to quilt. I've been quilting one day a week for two years, and my quilt is the next one.

"I love the work and being with those dear older women. The chairman of the circle is eighty-seven. The best part is that with the money they earn quilting they have supported different Korean and Indonesian orphans for years."

## BIBLE STUDY

Not all the reaching out should be physical. The church needs to do more than provide a Sunday morning or weekday Bible study for its elderly members, some of whom are thinking, "I can't" instead of "God can." The church has a responsibility to help the old to accept willingly their place in the Body of Christ, to consider death, and to hope in the life to come.

"I thought when I grew old," one woman said, "that Satan would no longer tempt me. But I found that is not true. As old as I am, God tests me. My tongue gets me into trouble, and I need to ask for forgiveness and repent."

If older church members are left without relatives or are in need, the church should assume responsibility just as surely as if a young child were left without support.

One large suburban church established an emergency fund for members, including the elderly, who face problems of housing, health, lack of income, or need for legal advice. The fund is administered by a committee.

Through the power-packed love of God, we can provide on-the-spot service to the elderly in the church pew. By showing them how to interact with all ages, we help them exercise their faculties, stretch their minds, and be a part of the church.

# 10

## THEY HELP THEMSELVES

"It's not how many years we live, but what we do with them," Evangeline Booth, former general and international leader of the Salvation Army, once said. Her statement appears to be the slogan of innumerable elderly persons.

People age at different times and in various ways. Some revert to apathy and discouragement soon after retirement, or they retreat into the past and complain, "We never did it that way before." Others possess optimism and self-reliance that keep them going full steam ahead to the close of life.

One couple in their eighties who had plans for the future told the salesman when they bought an automatic washer, "We hope the new washer lasts as long as the old one. We had it for twenty years."

A man in his late seventies declared, "Each day is a gift from God. I hadn't thought He would give me so many years. But He has. Each morning I step up to life as if it were a family reunion picnic, where I sample every potluck dish."

We see active couples over sixty-five working full or part time. Widows, who might otherwise be depressed or live in the past, have joined the work force. Others branch out into a second career after retirement. None of them wants to sit at home in a rocking chair, and they may need additional funds to supplement social security. Many go back to school to learn a new language or skill. They take courses to increase their knowledge of local and world affairs with a view to making their votes count.

Countless old persons put their efforts into volunteer work. Those who are curious about other parts of our country and the rest of the world, and who can afford it, find travel a means of keeping alert.

These lively elderly ones are helping themselves to a good old age in spite of disability and diminished reserve strength. Most of the old who are self-reliant have several things going for them. They take care of their health. They possess zest for living, curiosity about life, and expectancy for the future.

Gerontologists urge our country to make better use of the wisdom, stability, and integrity of the elderly by providing more jobs for those who want to work. If the old continue working even part time, many potential welfare recipients could be self-supporting, thus decreasing welfare costs and taxes, as well as lightening the financial burden on their children.

What some resourceful older persons have done to help themselves in the last third of a long life may encourage others to come up with ideas suited to themselves.

1. Frank and Hazel Addington had supported missionaries around the world for years. At retirement age, Frank sold his business. The Addingtons set out on a five-month world trip, visiting thirty missionary families they knew. Those they visited included a doctor son and his family, missionaries in Hong Kong; and a daughter and her family, missionaries in Lisbon, Portugal.

The Addingtons not only had the time of their lives, but they also gained new insight into the missionary enterprise. On returning Frank said, "All my life I've heard missionaries say they loved the people they worked with. I never understood that. Now I do."

After their return, Frank began work in a second career.

2. A retired schoolteacher works part time instructing pupils in remedial reading. She also teaches English to Vietnamese refugees and international university students.

3. When he reached sixty-seven, Elmer L. Andersen, former Minnesota governor, purchased two newspapers in a small town, taking on a new career. "Running a newspaper," he said, "is something I have had as a lifetime goal."

4. A seventy-year-old woman who has been an architect and contractor for many years is still hard at work, designing and building houses. She says, "It gets better every year."

5. Love of music led another man to find out all he could about organs while still working at an office job. He learned how to play an organ, and how to repair and build them. Well over retirement age, he and his son have been partners for years in a flourishing organ-building business.

6. After he retired, an executive built a part-time second career from his hobby of photography. He took a university course in photography and equipped a darkroom in his basement. Soon his work was in demand for confirmation classes, graduations, weddings, and church publicity.

7. Another man learned how to refinish and upholster furniture. He converted his basement into a shop and has more work than he can handle.

8. A widow who lives near the local veterans' hospital rents several rooms to those from out of town who visit patients. Her fee is modest. Guests take care of their own

rooms and beds. Before checking out they remake the bed with clean sheets, leaving it ready for the next guest.

The roomers are instructed not to come down for breakfast, a light "help yourself" meal, until after eight o'clock. The hour before breakfast is her time for prayer and Bible study. In the evening, she invites her visitors to her living room to watch television or talk over concerns they have about their loved ones in the hospital.

"This is your home away from home," the woman tells them. Often she serves a treat, such as homemade apple pie.

9. For a small remuneration some retirees work with the Foster Grandparent program, helping children mentally retarded, handicapped, emotionally disturbed, or delinquent. "Grandparents" are transported to the job and work about half time. Great improvement is noted—not only in the children, but in the grandparents as well.

10. Elderly, low-income, rural men and women work for Green Thumb, Inc., a public service employment program sponsored by the United States Department of Labor. Green Thumb employs the elderly to work on community improvement and conservation projects, and to help other aged shut-ins and handicapped. (See Appendix.)

11. Many spirited old people assume the responsibility of preserving a family's historical heritage through careful records, memoirs, and caring for family antiques. An eighty-year-old man researched and compiled his family's history. He had the material bound in booklet form, and then he presented one to each of his descendants, a valuable legacy.

12. A ninety-year-old woman in Texas learned to type and recently applied for a social security number.

13. Olga Soderberg collected historical objects in rural

northern Minnesota while still a county schoolteacher. After her retirement as county superintendent of schools, she worked to procure land and a building for the Cook County Historical Society in Grand Marais. Many valuable relics and artifacts of Minnesota's early history are housed in the museum.

14. Still other old people crusade to protect the environment and society for future generations. The Gray Panthers organization campaigns against age-based discrimination.

15. Going back to school is one way to keep an old mind active. Studies reveal that the ability to reason and absorb knowledge stays with us well past the seventies. It may, though, take longer for an old person to learn new subjects.

More than five hundred schools in the United States offer special courses or continuing-education programs. Some schools provide free tuition or reduced rates for those over sixty-five.

The elderly who want to add to their store of knowledge might study history—the Jews, religion, slavery, Indians, United States government, or the discovery of America. Samuel Eliot Morison has written a fascinating account: *European Discovery of America: The Northern Voyages* (New York: Oxford, 1971).

16. Immediately after retiring, a minister enrolled in an advanced electronics class by correspondence. Already a ham radio operator of long experience, he added to his knowledge of radio and television.

17. Many men and women enroll in intensive Bible study through correspondence courses or Bible school in that period of life when they are evaluating the past and what God means to them.

Someone once said to a radio pastor, "I wish I knew the Bible like you do."

71

The pastor replied, "If you study the Bible every day for fifty years, you will know it like I do." The old no longer have fifty years, but studying the Bible in the time left to them will bring not only knowledge but also a sense of God's direction.

Subscriptions to a news weekly, the daily newspaper, and one or two religious periodicals spark curiosity and interest in local and world affairs for many old persons. A popular aid for keeping alert to the activities and problems of the elderly is a subscription to the American Association of Retired Persons (AARP) publications. One is the colorful bimonthly *Modern Maturity,* the other a monthly bulletin. (See Appendix.)

These accounts of what some old persons are accomplishing will remain just examples and suggestions unless we encourage those who have grown old to pick them up and try them.

A speaker once said, "Our Lord Jesus Christ not only saves us from a dead-end life, but also from living a dead life." Alive—no matter how long they live!

# 11

## OUTLOOK FOR SHUT-INS

Elmer's daughter Karen settled him in the wheelchair near the window. She tucked an afghan around his legs, for he was just home from the hospital. When Karen smiled she reminded him of Martha. But Martha was gone, and he was seventy-five and useless.

"Take it easy for three months," the doctor had said. "No yard work. Get somebody in to take care of you."

Elmer looked out the window to the little apple orchard he had planted and then tended for years. The blossoms were beginning to open and there was work to do out there, but he was shut in for three months.

Anyone who reaches old age is likely to be shut in sooner or later for weeks or months, or even years. The disability, pain, and loneliness are hard to accept. Legs and arms will not perform as they formerly would. Thoughts cannot be expressed. It means extra work for others. Being shut away from former activities, one feels isolated and useless.

Except for the seriously brain-damaged, shut-ins need not settle for hibernation or for feeling grim and depressed. Instead, we can help them choose circulation, ways to be useful to others.

Elmer's son and daughter-in-law, who lived in another state, flew home to make plans for him. "Dad," his son said, "you should sell the place and move into Harmony Hills."

It certainly looked as though he would be better off moving to the home, where everything was bright and new and he would be cared for. Elmer sniffed the apple blossoms through the open window. Harmony Hills was a glorified old folks home on the edge of town, and he was not ready for that. So he said in a loud voice, "No!"

"Well, you don't want Karen to give up her job and stay home to take care of you," his son said. "You can't stay alone."

Of course he did not want Karen to give up her good job with the welfare board to take care of him. He scowled.

"Dad's not helpless," Karen said. She knew the quickest way for old people to decline is to settle down and let others take care of them. "He can do some things. We can get help for what he can't do."

After the others left, Karen brought her father a glass of warm milk. "Dad, don't make a quick decision. I'm working with a young woman with two children. Her husband ran off, and we can't locate him. She needs a home and a little money. She's willing to work where she can keep an eye on her children."

"Tell her to come out so we can get acquainted," Elmer said.

The thing that most helped Elmer on the road to recovery was the feeling that he was doing something worthwhile in giving the young divorcée and her children a home in return for her work. As time passed he did more and more for himself and the youngsters. He began to understand that God knows about every "step and stop" of His children, and that the present stop would not last forever.

Shut-ins need care and loving attention from others in

74

the household. It is often easier to be a Christian when things are going well than when one suffers great pain or is confined with nothing to do. Boredom may then result, and along with it increased complaining. Encouraging words will brighten dark days for the invalid.

"I hope you will receive half as much kindness and help from others as you have given in the past."

"You are as close to God shut in your room as in any other place you might be."

Those who must care for a bedridden or wheelchair patient in the home would profit by enrolling in a home nursing course. Often, though, the therapy that will benefit shut-ins the most is looking outward. As they discover ways to hearten or reinforce others, they will begin to feel useful and worthwhile.

Marcia helped her eighty-four-year-old aunt to a little independence. The elderly woman left the hospital after hip surgery to recuperate at Marcia's house. Marcia put everything her aunt would need during the night on a lazy Susan on the bedside table. At first the attempt to wait on herself through the night exhausted the invalid. Gradually she slept better as the result of such effort, and so did her practical nurse-niece, who did not forget to praise her aunt.

"Good for you, auntie. You didn't have to call me last night. I had a good night's rest, so we'll do something special today."

The following are just a few ways in which shut-ins can look outward.

LETTERS

Offer to write, or get a child in the family to write for those too feeble to do so. Those who write their own letters might consider writing to:

young people away at college
other shut-ins
church missionaries
new church members
children confined to the hospital
anyone in the church whose work is appreciated
teens committed to detention homes, or on parole
public officials who are making worthwhile efforts
worthy television programs

## TELEPHONE

A bedside phone or one with a long cord could lift an invalid out of boredom. The shut-in can answer incoming calls. The surprise of each ring will lighten the shut-in's day, and, in the event the caller merely wants to know how the invalid is doing, give minutes of free time to the one in charge.

By using a phone, shut-ins can be part of a prayer chain, a link in a publicity chain, or even a phone reassurance program.

A word of warning: active, busy people do not have time for lengthy calls. The shut-in should announce the purpose of the call and then cheerfully say good-bye. A chatty call may be in order when directed to other shut-ins or the lonely.

## HANDWORK

Those whose hands are steady may cut out magazine pictures of children, animals, scenes of water and land, or anything else that Sunday school teachers might use for stories and class projects.

One elderly woman confined to her home clipped poetry and epigrams from religious and secular magazines, pasting them in a small, bound booklet. As she completed each booklet, she sent it to someone in the hospital or another shut-in. When making such books it is wise to include the date of publication and name of each periodical from which the clippings came.

A variation would be to clip and paste jokes, puzzles, and riddles in a notebook to give to a child.

One elderly shut-in knitted mittens for children. Friends gave her leftover balls of yarn. When the fall season arrived, she handed the mittens to a third-grade teacher in a deprived school district. Then she began knitting mittens for the following season.

One grandmother, too frail to go out, patched jeans and mended clothing for her son's family of six, helping to stretch his paycheck. At times she sewed on buttons and mended for her minister's family.

### FAMILY RECORDS

With help, shut-ins might date and label photos they have saved that would otherwise become meaningless in time.

A man I read about made a valuable record for his family. He bought a sturdy scrapbook, chose representative photos of his family in the past, and pasted them on each page. Then he wrote a short description of the time, people, occasion, date, and meaning of each picture. The pictures came alive for his family in a permanent record.

A shut-in may provide oral tapes for descendants. To get the old person started, ask, "How did they used to do it when you were young?" Ask about colors, sounds, smells, and tastes to give grandchildren a glimpse into the past. The old one might include family recipes, or describe a now-famous event that occurred long ago.

77

Also interesting to descendants would be a statement of the old person's faith, a description of his conversion, and a description of what an old-time evangelistic meeting was like.

## BIBLE

One shut-in who has poor vision keeps her Bible open on a table beside her chair. She asks each visitor to read her a few verses or a chapter. She often helps her grandchildren memorize Scripture or the books of the Bible.

## PRAYER

Some never learn the confidence and joy that come from praying until late in life. Others have talked to God all their lives. Prayer is the means through which the Holy Spirit reveals God's will or calls an old one to repentance.

Keeping a notebook of others' prayer needs and answers will widen a shut-in's outlook.

A retired teacher uses a low oval table to display the graduation and wedding pictures of girls she formerly taught in Sunday school classes. She lays the pictures under glass around the rim of the table. Arthritis binds her to the house, but she travels across America in prayer.

A prayer activity that is made to order for shut-ins is praying for television and radio reporters and commentators, and for the betterment of network programs.

A woman who found out early in life that she would be a cripple says, "I prayed God would heal me. Instead He gave me courage never to let my affliction embitter me. He has allowed me to live a full, rich life, helping others."

A librarian can suggest books for the shut-in. Has the aged one longed to travel to another country—the Holy Land, New Guinea, Alaska? A shut-in can take an armchair trip to such places. *The National Geographic* magazine also carries fascinating reading of other cultures and lands. For those whose hands are too crippled to flip pages, there are mechanical page turners, overhead projectors, talking books, cassette tapes, and films on travel, nature, and events.

By trying to put ourselves in the place of a person who has had a stroke and imagining his frustrations, we may better understand his difficulties. After asking a question, wait. Let the person try to speak. Watch for nonverbal signs.

Perhaps these activities are beyond the strength of some shut-ins, but none are too weak and helpless to grasp the Saviour's outstretched hand. Loving-kindness will help them understand that as with Noah in the Bible, God has shut the door for a purpose. That purpose may be for healing or for a witness to the family of patience and trust in God, or even to allow the family to consider the meaning of old age and approaching death. It may be a time of meditation and getting ready to meet the Lord. A shut-in at home provides the rest of the family with opportunities for service and compassion.

# 12

# STARTING YOUNG

"My grandma listens to me," Dave, a junior high school student, said. "She doesn't hand out a lecture or a lot of Bible verses when I fall on my face.

"I used to think my dad was perfect when he was a boy. Grandma helps me see that no matter what age you are, you have problems and have to work at them."

Teenage Jan said, "My grandfather is fun. He laughs and tells these old jokes and unbelievable stories about what happened sixty years ago. He listens to me, too. And he never yells at me or gets nervous when I drive. He makes me feel like a person."

What Dave and Jan may not realize is that as they in turn listen to their grandparents, the old ones, too, feel loved and respected.

It is easy to honor grandparents when parents have sown the seeds for love and respect. Grandparents have brought presents; read endless stories; played games; and attended recitals, band concerts, and graduations. Grandparents have shown their love. They are part of the family. Love and respect are two-way.

But *old people*? What about those outside the family—those in church, and strangers? Not all young people are concerned about the elderly. Some do not care at all for older ones they do not know. They may even have negative feelings toward them.

"Old people have wrinkles. They're slow and ugly. They're sad," Linda said.

Dawn criticized a careless old man living down the block. "He's a mess. Needs a haircut. His clothes are rumpled and he smells."

Brian works as an orderly in a nursing home. "There's this old man. We get him in the wheelchair and he just sits all day. Won't answer when we talk to him, so we leave him alone."

At an anniversary celebration, two young women withdrew from a friend of mine. "I saw them across the room," she said, "and walked over to talk to them. They had grown up with my kids and had been in our house dozens of times. But I hadn't seen them for a long time. They looked at my white hair and simply didn't know what to say. I could see a light switch on in their heads as they labeled me 'old.' "

My friend's experience reminded me of the time in a group when I brought up the subject of how young people could help the aged. A young man shrugged. "I'm not at all interested in the subject," he said. "I don't intend to be old."

Can such attitudes be changed? Can children and young people learn to understand what it means to be old?

According to Bert Kruger Smith, delegates to the 1971 White House Conference on Aging (a conference held every ten years) stressed that since aging begins at birth, "knowledge about it should be part of the task of every age group." Courses on the physical, mental, and social aspects of aging should be taught in secondary schools.[1]

Long before school, parents can lay the groundwork for

consideration of the old by talking about the life cycle: birth, childhood, youth, middle age, old age, and death. They can help their children see the elderly not as one group but as individuals who have different physical, mental, and emotional characteristics.

Parents teach tenderness and thoughtfulness for others by their example. They teach by smiles and affectionate words to the old, by refraining from criticism or ridicule.

Connie, over seventy herself, has spent a lifetime helping older people. She says, "My mother taught me from little on to love and respect our elderly relatives and friends. It's second nature to me."

Children and young people with such parents are on the way to understanding the elderly. In turn, the elderly have a way of understanding the difficulties young people get into. After sixty or seventy years of coming to crossroads, they take a farsighted view of life. They have often wandered along the wrong road themselves and regretted mistakes. Old people who trust in Jesus Christ have a faith that is unshakable. That is important in this shaky world.

Anyone who knows old people realizes most of them cannot walk as far or as fast, or eat as much as the young. Even sprightly old people have learned to protect and conserve strength, to take care of their deteriorating bodies. It is therefore important to gear our help to their strength and speed.

Some mothers lead their children into thinking of older persons as a young mother does during summer vacation. Once a week she reads poetry and familiar books to several men and women who are nearly blind, living in a retirement home.

Her seven- and eight-year-old boys help settle the old ones in a circle. The boys shake hands and call them by name. The children are beginning to think of the elderly as a part of God's family.

A nurse helps her teenage daughters toward patience and concern for the elderly by occasionally taking them to the nursing home where she works. Acting as volunteers, the girls read to the patients, play games with them, write letters, or just talk and listen.

Children need not be quiet and tiptoe around the elderly who are ill. Authorities say that noise within reason is a connecting link between generations.

Mrs. Harrison, recovering from serious illness at her daughter's home, showed her pleasure when her daughter's neighbor brought her three preschool youngsters in for a visit. At first the children were shy and quiet, but soon they grew noisy.

"You're too noisy," their mother said. "We're going home."

"Their noise is music to my ears," Mrs. Harrison said. "Please come again."

That night when the oldest child was tucked into bed he told his mother, "It's too bad Mrs. Harrison has to stay in bed all day." The seed of compassion had been planted.

Noise may benefit an old person, but not jostling or pushing. The elderly are often unsure walking; their bones are brittle, and they stumble easily. What happened to one older woman should be avoided at all costs: a boy's foot carelessly outstretched in a restaurant caused her to trip, break an arm, and have to be hospitalized.

A teacher of primary-age children in a church day-school helped her pupils make friends with an elderly man in the neighborhood. Walking past the school every day, he often stopped and talked to the children as they played outside.

"Can you sing me a song?" he asked. Usually he found a

few pennies in his pocket to give to those who sang. The children soon called him Grandpa John.

Learning the date of his birthday, the teacher helped the class plan a birthday party for Grandpa John. They invited him into the schoolroom for songs and games and a birthday cake. The minister of the church came in, too, to welcome the man and give a birthday prayer.

"Best birthday I ever had," Grandpa John said.

High school students can learn about the aged by practical work assignments: in Red Cross first-aid courses; as volunteers and aides in nursing homes; and by driving the elderly to church functions and other activities.

Not long ago I watched a candy striper of about thirteen come up to a woman in a wheelchair and kiss her warmly on the cheek. "Mrs. Allen," she said, "I'm going to push you into the lounge. We'll sing old-time songs." Who could tell which smile was the brightest—Mrs. Allen's or the girl's?

As the number of those over sixty-five in our country increases, many job opportunities in the field will open up. Young people might consider preparing for a career in gerontology, geriatrics, psychiatric nursing, medicine, social services, or rehabilitation of the old.

A college student who wanted to make geriatrics her vocation worked as an aide in a nursing home one summer. While there, she learned that some old people need to be treated like children. Brain damage from strokes, malnutrition, or other illnesses can cause undesirable behavior.

Alma, a new patient, confused and lost in the hall, could not find her room. The aide told another patient, "Bertha, please show Alma where her room is."

Bertha turned her back. "Why should I?"

The aide took Bertha's arm. "Let's do it together." Bertha

walked along with a pout, and they showed Alma her room.

The college student aide also learned that a sense of humor is an asset when working with the aged.

Lester ran his wheelchair up and down the halls like a drag racer. Once he blocked the door of another wheelchair patient who wanted to come out of her room.

"Please move out of the way," she said.

"No." Lester refused to budge.

"Help!" yelled the woman.

The nurse's aide hurried to the fracas. "What's going on here?"

"He won't let me out."

"Move your chair, Lester," the aide said, giving him a shove in the other direction. Lester grinned and scooted off.

Gordy and Ardis, a young couple who moved from a small town to the city, showed their neighbor they cared about her.

Mrs. McGraw was over eighty, unsteady, nearly blind, and often confused. One day her back doorknob fell off in her hand. Gordy, who saw the situation, brought over a screwdriver and fixed the doorknob. He took a look around and noticed that other parts of her house also needed fixing.

"Look," he said. "I'll find time to fix anything you need done. Make a list so I can have it before me and work it into my schedule."

I find it heartwarming to read of the many ways young people are reaching out to the elderly. In some cities, youth patrols escort the old to stores, to the dentist, to the doctor or bank, or just to protect them. Young people who have no aged relatives nearby correspond with distant ones. Others grandma-sit for someone who is tied down with nursing cares.

Cindy lived with her great-grandmother one summer while working away from home. Her great-grandmother, nearly blind, was housebound. "I really got to know her," Cindy says, "and I love her very much."

While one woman was growing up, her grandmother lived with her family. Now married, the woman says, "I wish I had understood then how much older people appreciate attention. Even a five-minute visit or phone call makes their day."

Many old people have full schedules. Others have little or nothing to do, and to do nothing all day is very hard.

As those who are young make friends with the old and try to understand them, they will not only bring joy and hope to the aged but they will also begin to learn what it means to live the last part of the life cycle.

# 13

## FREEWILL OFFERING

My brother-in-law has discovered one secret of happy leisure years. Retired from a demanding executive position, he and my sister travel quite a bit, often visiting friends and older relatives.

"How are you enjoying retirement?" I asked.

"Fine. I'm doing a lot of things I always wanted to do." Then he added, "If a fellow runs out of things to do, he can always help others. I carry my toolbox with me wherever we travel."

Several widows had already told me of minor repairs he had made in a heating system in one house; on the plumbing, sagging screen doors, and broken steps in another.

He probably would not consider himself a volunteer, but others do. The cost for professional repairs would have been high.

No other freewill offering is quite like volunteer work. Whether we give to individuals or nonprofit organizations, it means giving part of ourselves. Many community health agencies would suffer without volunteer help. They depend on men, women, and teen volunteers from all walks of life—thousands and thousands of them across our land.

When we live in the midst of a lively family, we may think there is no time for volunteer work. "If you haven't time to do something," I once heard Paul E. Little say, "it's not because you don't have time, but because you don't consider it important."

Some hold back from volunteer work thinking they need special talent and training. Instead, working with the elderly requires a slice of time, a warm heart, and a willingness to listen. The volunteer who finds it easy to laugh and is sympathetic will discover that behind the lonely, frightened eyes and inside the frail body is a heart that never grows old.

Whether the volunteer work takes place in our homes, outside our homes, at community service agencies, or in institutions, a few suggestions from authorities and the experienced may help.

One gerontologist suggests volunteers should forget about helping the old in stereotypical ways: that is, in terms of their financial, physical, or social situations. Rather, think of them "where their heads are."

Etta Saloshin, a retired gerontologist in the University of Minnesota School of Social Work, says, "The mind is so alive that people shouldn't just use it to play bingo or take a boat trip down the river."[1] Volunteers can steer the aged toward activities that use the mind, including education and being informed on current events and world affairs. The importance of mental stimulation cannot be overestimated.

Many aged people are apathetic or like the woman with the frightened blue eyes who sat in a wheelchair in a nursing home with all her feelings bottled up inside. Recalling some of her past accomplishments may help her think of what she might be doing now.

Whenever the old complain about surroundings, food, relatives, or neighbors, repeat their statements to them. Charlie W. Shedd, in his book *Talk To Me*, advocates what he calls "say-it-back" talk. By "say-it-back" he means, "You encourage the flow. You invite him to keep coming on. The more you draw his negatives out of him, the better he will feel inside."[2]

Not everyone who reaches old age is mellow, mature, and lovable. Some are complainers, childish, and untidy. Those who gave advice in their forties are sure to boss others in their seventies and eighties. Those who lost their temper in youth may still have trouble controlling it in old age. A volunteer may need peacemaking abilities.

If one's schedule is actually too tight to allow a morning or afternoon for volunteer work with a nonprofit organization, bits and pieces of time can be used right at home. What some resourceful volunteers have undertaken may suggest activities for others.

### VOLUNTARY HELP FROM HOME

Pray for the elderly who call you on the phone—just a sentence or two after they hang up.

"Lord, give her the capacity to be patient."

"O God, give him wisdom in this thorny situation."

"Lord, in her pain and affliction, keep her trusting in Your strength."

Call one or two lonely old ones regularly to assure them of your love and concern. Take time to listen. Speak of subjects that will set the older ones thinking.

Instead of sending scores of Christmas cards to those we scarcely know, we can write a love letter full of family news to out-of-state, older relatives.

Write love notes of appreciation to the old ones nearby.

One Christmas season, a young woman wrote a note to her Bible teacher, who was older than she. "The year has been a better one for knowing you. In your class I've learned to trust the Saviour." The teacher knew the young woman had crossed the threshold to a new spiritual experience, but hearing it from the young woman encouraged the teacher.

Most of us help an elderly neighbor or two on occasion. We shovel the snow, cut the grass, bake cookies, and provide rides for grocery shopping or to church. There are also other pressing needs. The following ad appeared in a city newspaper column titled "They Need You."

> Needed a Friend—Three hours, once a week to visit with the elderly in a senior high-rise apartment. To act as a liaison between residents and other social agencies providing services. Men and women needed.

Carrie is one who takes an interest in the elderly, escorting women to their doctors and dentists, or on shopping trips. She repairs clothing and adjusts hems, and reads letters and writes checks for those with failing eyesight.

"I try to find out what older people are interested in," Carrie says. "One woman likes to press flowers, so I pick garden and wild flowers for her hobby."

Older volunteers might check out the Retired Senior Volunteer Program (RSVP). Over ninety thousand retired persons are enrolled in RSVP. The program lists the talents and skills of those over sixty and refers them to local service agencies in need of part-time volunteers. Jobs undertaken by RSVP volunteers include repairing toys and library books, teaching skills, mending, serving as aides, and phoning housebound old ones. (See Appendix.)

High on the list of volunteer work stands that of teachers who have elderly ones in Bible classes. Experience shows that old ears must strain to catch words and that stiff and shaking hands are slow to turn the thin pages of a Bible. Some need to be taught at the junior high school level. Others who are quick and knowledgeable may monopolize the discussion. Those who are garrulous may talk about irrelevant matters. Both need kindly restraint.

Many older Christians are no more faithful about prayer and Bible study than many younger ones. They do, though, have more time, and may be stimulated to use it.

### VOLUNTARY WORK IN A HOSPITAL

The "pink lady" walked into room 317. "How are you?" she asked the patient who was scheduled for surgery.

"I'm scared," the woman replied. "The nurses and doctors are so busy I don't like to ask them what to expect."

The "pink lady" had undergone surgery some time ago, so she explained to the woman what she might expect. Still she looked fearful.

"Would you like me to pray for you?"

"Oh, yes," the woman said. The prayer helped her relax.

### VOLUNTARY WORK IN A NURSING HOME

Those who offer their services to the program director of a nursing home may volunteer for as little as an hour or two a week, or for as much time as they can give.

One young woman who applied as a volunteer returned to her family almost in shock. "They gave me the names of three patients who never have visitors. Nobody! I'm going to let some things go around here and spend time with those old people every week."

Reading Scripture and praying can bring comfort to the very old and feeble. We need to be sensitive, though, to their lack of strength. One woman, terminally ill, said when a volunteer asked if she might read a psalm, "Yes, if it's very short." The volunteer changed her plan and repeated the first verse of the twenty-third psalm and a sentence prayer. With closed eyes the woman managed a small smile, and the volunteer left the room.

## OTHER PROGRAMS THAT NEED VOLUNTEERS

Day centers; senior citizen groups that provide hot meals and teach handcraft, knitting, sewing, painting; and the public library—all depend on volunteer aid.

The American Association of Retired Persons (AARP) sponsors many good voluntary programs. Last year volunteers in AARP's Tax-Aide Program helped more than 305,000 older Americans file their returns.

The AARP's Generations Alliance Program functions with the "aim to bridge any gap that may exist between young and old." Camp Fire Girls, 4-H clubs, Girl Scouts, American Red Cross Youth Service, and others take part. AARP members join with the younger groups in discussions, and may teach their skills to the younger ones. (See Appendix.)

The Salvation Army in Minneapolis received a federal grant to operate the Congregate Dining Project in Hennepin and Anoka counties. The program's director, Col. T. Herbert Martin, states, "Without volunteers this program couldn't function. At least fifty volunteers from churches and other groups serve each day of the five-day week."

A woman who has freely given hundreds of hours to volunteer work says, "I think of it as a memorial to my parents."

I like the spirit of the volunteer in her eighties who said, "I've made my reservation in the heavenly high-rise, and it's rent free. In the meantime I want to do for others until I die. That way somebody will miss me when I'm gone."

Whether they will be missed or not, volunteers do not wait to be asked. They plunge right in and offer a part of themselves.

# 14

# DON'T GIVE GRANDPARENTS ROLLER SKATES

Roller skates for Grandpa or Grandma? Nobody would give such an inappropriate gift. Nobody would plan a roller skating party for the elderly. Or would they?

Some of the gifts old ones receive from well-meaning friends and relatives are about as farfetched as roller skates. Social affairs, picnics, parties, and family get-togethers often fail to consider the abilities and interests of the old, forcing them to be onlookers and not participants.

What happened to Mrs. Andrews one Christmas would never have occurred if her three daughters had consulted her and one another. Three large boxes under the Christmas tree, addressed to "Mom" and adorned with red and gold ribbons, contained three elegant robes. Mrs. Andrews already had a warm robe. She did want, but could not afford, wool long johns (though she never would have called them that). Poor circulation plus having the thermostat set at sixty-eight degrees in her daughter's home where she lived meant Mrs. Andrews shivered most of the time.

Mrs. Stebbins easily choked on nuts because of a goiter operation. Yet every Christmas one of her friends brought her a box of salted almonds. "They're my favorite," the giver said.

Bursitis in his shoulder made it impossible for Joe to raise his arms shoulder-high. His chest of drawers held several pairs of unused pajamas with slipover tops, gifts from his children. He could have managed the button-down-the-front kind, but not the slipovers.

Appropriate gifts or parties for the old require thought. The longer people live, the more simple their wants. In the last part of a long life, the old usually see material things as temporary and unimportant. Still, like all of us, they have needs and enjoy gifts and parties.

The gift many old ones really want is money. Not five hundred or a thousand dollars, but five or ten dollars to spend any way they choose.

## LIGHTHEARTED WAYS TO GIVE MONEY

1. Create a money tree from a bare lilac branch or small tree. Spray the branch gold or silver and set it in a jar of wet sand. Pleat dollar bills and tie them on with bright ribbons.

2. Fashion a money doll, using crisp, pleated bills for skirt and arms, and a coin for the face.

3. Stuff a ceramic piggy bank with bills and coins.

4. Sew a little drawstring bag and fill it with coins.

5. Put folded bills in an envelope along with a picture of a suggested way to spend it—books, records, plants, needlework, or materials for some hobby.

6. Tuck a supply of postage stamps and a ball-point pen in a box of notepaper.

7. Tickets for a concert or ballgame should be accompanied by a promise of transportation the night of the event.

## LAVISH GIFTS

Consider giving a radio, television, stair elevator,

motorized wheelchair, talking record player, airplane ticket, or a phone for the old person's bedside.

## FOR THE HOUSEBOUND

1. If the elderly one is confined to bed, a hospital table or backrest would be useful. A tray on legs or a small teapot might also be of service.

2. A housebound old person will probably enjoy a bouquet of garden snapdragons and zinnias more than a costly arrangement left over from a funeral.

3. One woman buys narcissus bulbs in December, sets them in bowls with pebbles, and carries them to shut-in friends. The shut-in can watch the bulbs grow. In six weeks the fragrant blossoms will signal hope to the one confined at home.

4. Many elderly people enjoy having their own copy of the daily newspaper so they can take their time reading it. Welcome, too, is a subscription to a denominational magazine or *Moody Monthly.*

5. A hymnbook with familiar church hymns can provide a worshipful experience in spite of a raspy throat.

6. Finding appropriate gift and greeting cards to send to the elderly may take time. Most cards are more blithe than sympathetic. "Hope you'll soon be well" needs to be replaced with words that bring comfort and understanding. Whenever she finds such cards, one woman buys a supply of them to use from time to time.

## PARTIES

Parties for the elderly should be short and simple. Refreshments, too, should be simple and eye-catching—not disturbing to older digestive systems. A blue bowl of chicken soup with the fat skimmed off may be more welcome than a three-layer chocolate cake with rich frosting. When planning parties for the old, try to include old friends, children, and young people.

Parties mean more when the honored guests are not allowed to sit on the bench but are pulled into things. They will enjoy themselves as they in effect pick up the ball and recall past celebrations, or take part in old-fashioned activities such as word games, charades, or a sing-along.

## CONDUCTED TOURS

Every fall when the leaves turn color, one high school youth group plans an outing for the elderly men and women of their church. With two young people in each car, they call for their passengers. Then, handling the cars as though trying to pass their driver's test, they tour points of interest in the city. The climax is a three-mile drive along the Mississippi River banks, whose trees appear aflame with red and yellow leaves. Afterward the women of the church serve a hot meal to the young people and their guests.

## HOUSE PARTY

Another youth group, besides caroling for the elderly during the Advent season, also plans an annual winter party for them. The young people separate into groups of two or three for an hour or so, calling on assigned housebound old ones.

The visitors sing, play musical instruments, read aloud from the Bible, play games, or ask the old people questions about the past. Calls on those who are ill should be short. A bright smile and hello, with someone reciting a psalm, will be enough.

After the home calls, the young people return to the church for cocoa and doughnuts. Then they talk over their experiences.

"Seeing those old people so content and cheerful makes me feel old age isn't going to be all bad," Jim said.

"They're fun to listen to," Adelle said. "They tell these corny jokes and laugh and treat you like you're important."

## Birthday Party

The women's circle of one church holds an annual birthday party. Younger women make arrangements to call for the older ones who need transportation. One year, after a program of special music, group singing, and an interesting speaker, the treasurer stood up, waving a tape measure. "Before refreshments I'm going to measure your waistlines." The women had already been asked to bring as many pennies, nickles, or dimes as they had inches around their waist.

Laughter and teasing accompanied the measuring. Those in charge used the money to buy birthday presents for the workers in a children's orphanage the church supported.

## Christmas Party

Early in December, when Donna had baked the Christmas cookies and decorated the house, she planned a party for her seventy-four-year-old mother who lived with her. Donna mailed invitations to several of her mother's friends, including their daughters and granddaughters.

As the guests arrived, Donna handed each a corsage of evergreens, tied with red ribbon. Then she made the older women comfortable in the living room before the blazing fireplace. One granddaughter played Christmas carols while the rest sang. Another girl read the Christmas story of Jesus' birth. Earlier, Donna had asked four of the elderly guests, each with a different national background, to tell how they had celebrated Christmas in their childhood. The younger women especially enjoyed hearing the accounts. One recorded the stories on tape.

Then the guests walked into the dining room, where they found their places around a decorated table. Donna knew that old people find it easier to sit at a table rather than manage a plate and cup on their laps.

The following year at the Christmas party, the women listened to the tape made the previous year, which became a valuable bit of history.

## SURPRISE PARTY

Half a dozen friends of one housebound woman surprised her on a dull November day. (They did let the one she lived with know they were coming.)

After visiting awhile the leader said, "It's time for a game." She quoted a line from several well-known hymns, and not always the first line. The person who named the hymn first scored a point. The prize was a slim book of favorite hymns.

Next, one of the visitors told the story behind one hymn and another sang it as a solo.

The party concluded with hot tea and cookies, provided by the guests, who left the kitchen in good order.

## GOING-AWAY PARTY

One time my mother was packed and ready to take an airplane to California to visit a son and his family for the winter. But the plane did not leave until the next noon, and the evening stretched ahead, making her fidgety.

The doorbell rang and in walked another son and his family, who lived nearby.

"We've come to have a going-away party," my sister-in-law said. She had made a cake, decorating it with a toy airplane and flags bearing the names of cities along the route to California. The children were as excited as their grandmother and made her promise to write all about the plane trip.

Because her family had made her feel important, she forgot to be nervous and enjoyed a good night's rest.

By taking thought, we can come up with suitable gifts tied in with the older person's desires or needs. By planning parties that consider the elderly's strength and interests, we show them we want to please them, and that we consider them important.

# 15

# SPECIAL PROBLEMS

One day when I "dialed a prayer," I heard the recorded words of Robert Dickson, minister of Hope Presbyterian Church, Richfield, Minnesota. "God's purpose in allowing any problem to come into our lives," he said, "is to have us admit our own weakness. Before He can help He has to hear us say, 'I'm licked, Lord. Help!' "

The elderly who are blind, deaf, incapable of driving, or senile have all been driven to the brink. If we were in their position, most of us would cry out, "I'm licked, Lord. Help!"

### BLIND

Blessed with sight, we can scarcely imagine what blindness is like. A sunrise or sunset; a star-strewn, purple sky; pale green leaves of spring; cornstalks tasseling; city buildings; the expression on a loved one's face—all these are denied sightless persons.

But sightlessness is never the end of things, as blind John Milton demonstrated. In *Paradise Lost*, Milton depicted Satan as saying:

> The mind is its own place, and in itself
> Can make a heav'n of hell, a hell of heav'n.

John Milton's great faith in the sovereignty of God enabled him to write of heaven on earth. Faith in God also sustained many other blind men and women. Louis Braille and Fanny Crosby turned their affliction into something heavenlike. Lesser-known blind ones, too, have risen above their "thorn in the flesh." Through the imagination and courage of all these, the blind and those with failing eyesight now receive many helps and services.

What would it be like to pull a Bible toward you, flip its pages, and not be able to read the words? The American Bible Society produces a complete braille Bible of eighteen volumes costing about $130.

Reading about the huge Bible, an eighty-two-year-old woman sent a check for $130. "My eyesight is good," she wrote. "In gratitude to God I want to provide the braille Bible for someone you choose who cannot see."

Compassion for those who cannot see led the women of a garden club to plant a fragrance garden on the property of the National Federation of the Blind in St. Paul, Minnesota. The fragrance garden includes a birdbath and benches for resting. The garden club chose plants with distinct fragrances and textures, and shrubs that would attract birds.

Some ways to help the elderly discussed in earlier chapters will also work for those who have failing eyesight or are blind. And other means of help are available.

The Library of Congress Division for the Blind and Physically Handicapped (Washington, D.C. 20542) provides talking records, brailled books, and other services postage free. Local libraries and organizations for the blind furnish many services and aids.

Helps range from a metal guide for signing personal checks (with in-home instructions) to brailled magazines and cassette tapes. All major magazines publish braille editions and also record "talking magazines," available below cost to the blind. The American Telephone and Telegraph Company issues a braille edition of its annual report. The Social Security Administration will accept letters written in braille and will reply in braille in some areas. Baseball schedules are available, as well as a braille handbook for basic fashions.

For those with failing eyesight, major magazines and some big-city newspapers publish large-print editions. *The Upper Room* devotional booklet and many books are printed in large type. Illuminated magnifying hand glasses are available.

Acquainting blind persons with any of these services or helping them toward acceptance of their affliction will bring "light" into their darkness. Mark Twain reminded us that one language the blind can read is kindness.

## DEAF

Kindness is also a language the deaf can hear. Comprehending the isolation of the deaf is difficult for those who can hear. A great chasm stretches between us, and we have no idea how to bridge it. But there are ways.

One hard-of-hearing man complains that his wife turns her back or goes out of the room and talks to him. "No wonder I can't hear her," he says. "If people would speak slowly and directly to me, I could get more of what they say."

Authorities are striving to inform us how we may be of help. In 1975, the World Federation of the Deaf, meeting in Washington, D.C., took steps toward the goal of preventing deafness. Delegates launched a worldwide program to immunize against diseases that cause deafness. In addition, committees stressed that rehabilitation programs should include use of leisure time. It was also noted that ways need to be developed to communicate to the deaf those emergency warnings that are ordinarily televised.

Not all those with hearing loss can be helped with hearing aids or even surgery. Those who become deaf late in life may learn to read lips. We can help, as noted earlier, by speaking face-to-face. Authorities say the deaf read not only lips, but also facial expressions. In one experiment, the face was covered except for the lips, and deaf students were unable to read the lips. The more of the face that was exposed, the easier it was for them to read.

Sign language is another help for the deaf. The Billy Graham Crusades provide an "interpreter" who relays the sermon in sign language to the deaf, who sit together in one section. Those who teach sign language say it is easy to learn. Very young children of deaf parents learn it quickly. The hand signals represent objects and ideas, not English words.

A traveling college choir from the Ozarks, "Sounds of Silence," sings, and at the same time "signs" the songs for the deaf.

Many churches have Bible classes for the deaf and those with hearing impairment.

We can help the deaf take special precautions. Keep doors locked. The doorbell should buzz loudly in all parts of the house. The phone company can install an extraloud bell or a light on the phone.

Anything we do to help the elderly deaf use their leisure time will lessen their isolation. They may even be of service to other old ones.

An elderly woman, totally deaf, sums up the problem and the answer. "It's a lonely, silent world I live in. At first, sounds were jumbled, blurred, but now sounds are almost completely lost. When a dear one looks at me, smiles, touches me, I understand though I cannot hear."

## UNSAFE DRIVER

Sooner or later, every old driver must face the question: *Should I retire from the road?* Good vision, quick reactions, skill, and proper attitudes all play a part in safe driving. When any of these fade, it is time to think about that question.

Age alone does not disqualify a driver. California reports 310 licensed drivers who are over ninety years old. Now and then we read of older drivers who realize their limitations and voluntarily give up the independence of driving. Thousands of others are still driving who have no business being behind the wheel.

Those who are concerned about the driving ability of an old person might suggest one or more of the following ideas.

1. Encourage older drivers to keep abreast of new highways and traffic laws. Many older adults now driving never took a driver's training course or a test because forty or fifty years ago, training and tests were not required. As a result, poor or careless driving habits learned years ago when traffic was light now handicap some older drivers.

A driver's refresher course or a defensive driver's course, sponsored by the National Safety Council, would underscore the capability of good drivers and pull dangerous ones off the road.

2. The older driver might ask his doctor, "Am I up to the demands of today's traffic?" Some physical conditions and medicines affect the driver's skill and judgment.

3. After reaching age sixty-five, night driving should be curtailed. Insurance companies remind us that the eyes of

older drivers tend to react slowly and fail to adapt quickly to changes in light.

I gave up night driving recently because of a form of night blindness that makes it difficult to react to oncoming lights and to see people or objects along the highway. I did not want to put myself in a situation where an accident would be inevitable.

4. An elderly driver should avoid peak traffic hours, stormy weather, and icy or snowy streets.

5. Be sure the older driver's car is in first-class condition—brakes, tires, lights, and everything under the hood.

The danger in his or her continuing to drive a car may be apparent to everyone but the aged driver. That is understandable. No one wants to give up the freedom and independence a car represents. In such circumstances, the family or interested others must step in and make the decision.

A young man in a family considering such a decision for his eighty-four-year-old grandmother said, "She still drives a car, but we're going to take that away from her. She's a slow driver. In the city, she could never make it, but even in her little town she's a hazard to other drivers."

On a visit to his aged parents who lived in a small town, a man rode with his father. He noticed the old man's poor driving habits.

"Dad," he said, "you almost hit that tree."

"Don't tell me how to drive," the father sputtered angrily. "I've been driving longer than you."

The son visited his father's doctor and explained his fear. "Your father should not be driving," the doctor said. "His physical condition rules out safe driving, and the medication he's taking is an added danger."

Fortified by the doctor's statement, the son visited the

sheriff, with the result that his father's license was not renewed. The old man transferred his antagonism to the sheriff instead of to his well-loved son, who was trying to help him.

The hazards of driving in today's traffic are already too great to permit unskilled driving or to overlook the dangers of poor judgment. Persuading an elderly one to give up driving when he or she is no longer competent is no small achievement.

Senility is the intellectual and emotional impairment caused by organic brain damage. It should not be confused with normal aging (slowing down of reactions and lack of interest, due mostly to habits of inactivity), nor with emotional disturbances that may occur in younger persons as well.

Some old persons labeled "senile" may not be. For example, in an old person, anemia or a heart that is too weak to pump blood to the brain can cause senile behavior. The same is true of thyroid disturbances, malnutrition, alcoholism, misuse of medication, and other conditions.

In his book *Why Survive? Being Old in America,* Robert N. Butler, M.D., says,

> Some of what is called senile is the result of brain damage. But anxiety and depression are also frequently lumped within the same category of senility, even though they are treatable and often reversible. Old people, like young people, experience a full range of emotions, including anxiety, grief, depression and paranoid states. It is all too easy to blame age and brain damage when accounting for the mental problems and emotional concerns of later life.[1]

Many persons find themselves in tight corners where they must make decisions and care for an older relative or friend who has suffered brain damage and shows senile behavior.

The counsel of their doctor enabled one family to work with a grim situation. After their father suffered extensive brain damage from a stroke, the doctor told them what behavior they could expect. He then stood by, giving some education, training, and encouragement to the family. When the time came, he helped them admit they had reached the end of their resources in the family home, necessitating a change of living arrangements for the father.

Dr. Harley J. Racer, who teaches family practice medicine at the University of Minnesota, says, "All effective approaches to understanding and caring about and for the senile must be based on a sensitive, comprehensive approach.

"For each older person who becomes senile, careful observation of capabilities by skillful counselors, psychologists and therapists can help family members work out with the physicians the best possible plans and expressions of caring love."

Sometimes friends and family together can help old ones understand their limitations. A middle-aged businessman, sensitive to his mother's need for supervision and protection, sought help from a longtime family friend.

"The doctor says Mother has suffered some brain damage and should not live alone," he said. "Could you persuade her to look at that new retirement center?"

"I'll try," Martha replied. When she talked to her friend, she found the woman on the defensive.

"My son and daughter-in-law want me to go to a mental hospital for psychiatric treatment," she said. "They say I forget to turn off the stove, that I don't know how to take care of my money, and I shouldn't live alone in this big house. They worry about me. They make me feel all shriveled up." Then she peered at her friend. "Martha, do you think they are right? Am I mental?"

"They don't want to put you in a mental hospital," Martha said. "They love you and want what's best for you. You do leave the burners on, and you told me about the trouble you have with your checkbook." Martha held her breath. "Your son wants you to consider that luxurious new retirement center. You would have meals served to you. Shall we look at it? Then you can make up your own mind."

The woman agreed. After inspecting the rooms and talking over the move with her son, she made the decision. Now she has new friends and still enjoys a measure of independence, while her son is assured of her supervision and protection.

One way we deprive the slow or confused elderly of their independence is by misplaced concern. By doing for them what they can readily do for themselves, we show them we think they are awkward or incapable. Instead, we need to approve and support their efforts. We also need to spend time with them and show our love.

Even those out of touch with reality benefit from attention and visits from loved ones. A frail old woman, helpless and brain-damaged from a stroke, began to cry whenever her daughter came to see her. The daughter told the head nurse, "I'm not coming so often. All she does is cry. I want to remember her alive and cheerful."

The nurse helped the daughter understand the crying spells were the result of brain injury. She also pointed out that the daughter's visits were the light in her mother's dark days. Gradually the daughter understood that just being there helped not only her mother but herself as well.

"Activities should emphasize the personhood of the old one," says Dr. Racer. "This means above all courtesy. The worst faults are speaking in a loud voice to one who is not deaf and talking down to a brain-injured person. Courtesy demands we use short sentences, and simple words.

"The key is the individual's level of ability. Loving such a person means sustaining that level at a maximum."

Depending on the degree of impairment, some of the following activities may be tried.

1. Let them touch and look at objects that will remind them of reality. I once took some brass bells from my collection to a nursing home. I explained a little of the history and meaning of each bell, then passed them to the wheelchair-bound residents. Some laughed and rang the bells with zest. Two squabbled over keeping one bell until an aide settled the skirmish.

2. Provide a large calendar so the aged one can cross off each day.

3. Help them enjoy God's world and the beauty all around them—trees, flowers, plants, and birds.

4. Get them to talk about their experiences, not their aches and pains.

5. If they are alert enough, help them read and listen to the news. Then get them to reflect aloud on what they have read and heard.

6. Suggest they do something for others, no matter how small the service.

7. Make sure their spiritual needs are met through chapel, radio or television church services, Bible reading, and prayer. Help them talk about God's grace, and open their eyes to the future.

8. For those who are disoriented, ask such questions as: "What is your name?"

"Who am I?"

"What day is it?"

"What year were you born?"

"What is the weather like outside?"

"What is the next meal?"

As we reach out to the senile or brain-damaged, or to the confused and forgetful persons in our family, neighborhood, or church, we will overcome our own prejudices and misunderstandings about senility. By showing love and concern, we may help them to respond.

# 16

# GETTING READY FOR TOMORROW

Snow had been falling since early morning. By afternoon, four inches of white feathers covered the sidewalk and driveway. Still drifting down, the snow looked as though it would keep falling all night.

Jeff considered going out to shovel. He knew his job was to clear the driveway before his father returned from work. "What's the use?" he told himself. "It's still snowing."

A what's-the-use attitude about their own old age grips countless young people and many who are not so young. Life will continue as it is. Old age appears far down the road and way around the corner. They cannot imagine being sixty-five. But time has a way of jetting us from here to there—the future of young people is old age.

All of us are hurtling toward that period of life. Tomorrow is closer than we imagine, as my friend has written:

I turned the calendar to June
And found December on the next page.

This book has stressed helping the elderly in various situations. But there is one old person we have overlooked. That is *you*—ten, twenty, or thirty years ahead.

Now that is an old one you should help!

What do today's youth or middle-aged want for themselves when they are old? What have they planned for that tomorrow?

A split-level house with a paid-off mortgage?
An A-frame in the north woods?
Money to retire in style?
Unlimited leisure?
Keeping even with expenses?

Do plans depend on a credit card? True, financial security in old age smooths the way to independence and brings many satisfactions within reach. It makes possible travel, adequate living facilities, and medical care, plus the ability to make generous contributions to the church.

What will it take to be financially secure in old age? That is a conundrum that worries many young people today. "As people prepare for old age," a young man told me, "they also should prepare for the shock of what may be ahead. The social security taxes I and millions like me pay now are taking care of our parents' social security payments.

"I don't begrudge it. I'm glad they are getting it. But a lot of us are thinking of that future shock. The money may not be there when we are old. If it is I'll be surprised."

Our government is already trying to put together the pieces of that puzzle.

At the same time, financial security is not everything. Mental, physical, and spiritual plans are also important. Financial goals may be meaningless without a strong attempt to grow as a person while still young.

Currently, those who retire receive five extra days a week. One who has failed to acquire skills and knowledge and to expand interests during a lifetime of work, will find retirement a letdown.

"At first," said a man retired more than ten years, "my wife and I traveled all over America and to other countries. Then old age and illness caught up with both of us: stiff joints, loss of hearing, and other ailments. A lot of folks where we live sit glued to television. Not us. We're interested and curious about our government, our relatives and friends across the country, and what's going on in the world.

"My wife and I like to read and learn. We read aloud or to ourselves. If I live to be one hundred I'll never read everything I want to."

To grow as a person, one needs to cultivate the habit of reading. Do it!

Preparation for tomorrow should include taking care of one's health. Good health in old age is an asset. As Bert Kruger Smith puts it in *Aging in America,* there should be "more emphasis in youth on the gift and protection of a healthy body."[1]

As I talked to the elderly I learned that what gives them security in old age more than anything else is trust in God—not money, things, or even people.

I have learned, too, that women live longer than men, so there are far more elderly women than couples.

Do young people want something better for themselves than what the old who are living today have? Consider what is being done in such areas as:

Social security benefits
Health services
Nursing homes
Transportation
Recreation
Continuing education
Congregate dining

114

Is enough being done? What disturbs or angers us? How these questions are dealt with will help determine the future for a great many people still working. A starting point in dealing with these issues might be to increase the number of old persons you know. Begin now with relatives, neighbors, and the elderly in church, and try to understand their needs. Try working as a volunteer in any of the previously named programs. Strive to change others' poor attitudes, policies, and values relating to the aged.

Love for and trust in family and friends are important in old age. The art of keeping friendships in repair and making new friends can be established while young. No one ever outgrows the need for friends. As Henry Van Dyke reminds us, "A friend is what the heart needs all the time."[2]

Investigate what the church is doing for the elderly. Henry Jacobsen, an authority on the aged, declares,

> The local church program of adult education must go beyond ministering to the needs of older men and women. It should help all adults, regardless of age, to accept with grace and confidence their place in the life cycle.
>
> It must train those in each group to respect the positions of those below them and above them—those who will someday replace them and those whom they will one day replace.[3]

Why wait until joints begin to creak before making plans for that tomorrow—old age? Wise people begin in youth and middle age to plant the seeds for a good harvest. They come to grips with their own old age and accept it as a gift from a wise and loving Father-God. They nurture curiosity and interest in progress and people. They reach out to the elderly.

What we do for today's aged will cost us money, time, and effort. Such effort takes a tenderized heart. But those who assume risks will be preparing for their own tomorrow. They will be growing as persons. They will also receive unexpected awards from the experts in lifetime living.

# 17

## EXPERTS IN LIFETIME LIVING

A father dashed back into his burning house because one of his little sons was missing. In the raging furnace that once was his home, he found the boy and rescued him. Then the father collapsed, burned to death. He gave his life for his child.

Such bravery makes headlines. A tragedy!

To give one's life to others through seventy, eighty, or ninety years takes bravery, too, but it may not reach the headlines. A victory?

Living through the heat of a lifetime often fires the elderly with knowledge and insight unknown in youth. They become experts in reaching sound conclusions and making wise decisions.

A wise man once said, "All of us are too old for some things, but no one is too old for all things." The special knowledge of the old has to do with wisdom, advice, patient endurance, wit, love, and service.

Old people are everywhere. All the while we are helping them they are doubtless, in hidden ways, helping us. Let them.

As the years have gone by, they have learned to know the Saviour better. With time to think and contemplate, they often brighten our days by distributing the fruit of the Spirit:

Love, joy, peace,
longsuffering,
gentleness,
goodness,
faith, meekness, temperance (Galatians 5:22-23).

In their old age, they know what it means to be indwelt by God's Spirit.

From the experts in lifetime living we learn to keep a loose hold on things. An alert, active octogenarian said, "I'm counting up life's simple joys, not stock certificates in the safety box. A well-cooked meal, tomatoes and beans growing in the garden, walking. Ah! the joy of walking! My Labrador beside me, yapping at strangers, greeting children."

An elderly woman, formerly well-off but now with little income, said, "I live in one room, so I don't have a house crowded with things, or closets overflowing with clothing. Instead, I'm holding on to remembered love and tenderness. I'm holding on to the promises of God."

"The godly . . . are transplanted into the Lord's own garden, and are under his personal care" (Psalm 92:12-13, TLB).

Elderly Christians inspire us with their strong convictions. They agree with the poet Henry Wadsworth Longfellow, who wrote that the best thing we can do when it rains is to let it rain. God's hand is in everything, they remind us, thus calling up our best reserves in stormy times.

One time I wrote a letter for a housebound woman with strong convictions who could no longer see to write. Friends had sent her an invitation to their daughter's wedding. Of course the invalid could not go to the wedding, but being remembered had flooded her day with light, and she wanted to write to the bride.

"I hope you have a beautiful wedding," she dictated. Then she added, "And a lasting one." She looked up. "I wonder if I should put that in?" She sat thinking aloud. "I don't like the way so many marriages break up." After a bit she said, "Leave it in."

Other experts in lifetime living inspire us with their faith. A woman dear to me who lives far away had been ill.

"Is there anything you need," I asked, "or that I can do?"

"There isn't anything anyone can do," she replied. "The Lord is taking good care of me, and I am blessed with contentment."

Many old ones delight us with their wit and humor. A wheelchair patient I sometimes visit often feels pain. One day I asked her if she was too ill for me to talk to her.

She shook her head. "I like to listen to you. I learned long ago that I could bore others by talking too much, but you never bore anybody by listening." Her eyes crinkled with laughter.

Laughing with her, I said, "What about me? Will I be boring you?"

"No," she said. "Please talk about your family. I like to listen."

Even those who are impatient and crotchety teach us pointed lessons about patience as we wait on them.

I do not agree with the writer who calls old age the only period of life without a future. The future of old age, for those who are true Christians, is life everlasting.

The experts, the strong ones, whose trust in the Saviour has grown through the years, have knowledge younger ones need.

Longfellow wrote:

> For age is opportunity no less
> Than youth itself, though in another dress,

And as the evening twilight fades away
The sky is filled with stars, invisible by day.

As those who are younger reach out to the elderly, they,
too, may find those stars.

# APPENDIX

For more information about help that is available, check the telephone directory or write state or federal offices of the following organizations and programs. Although non-Christian organizations, they perform valuable services for the elderly.

ACTION/RSVP (Retired Senior Volunteer Program—includes Foster Grandparent Program)
Washington, D.C. 20525

ACTION/RSVP
Office on Aging or Governor's Council on Aging
State Capital

American Foundation for the Blind
15 W. Sixteenth St.
New York, NY 10011

Green Thumb
1012 14th St., N.W.
Washington, D.C. 20005

Institute of Lifetime Learning
American Association of Retired Persons
1909 K St., N.W.
Washington, D.C. 20049
For membership, $3 per year, which includes bimonthly *Modern Maturity* and bulletin, write:
  AARP
  215 Long Beach Blvd.
  Long Beach, CA 90801

Large Print Book Club
G. K. Hall & Co.
70 Lincoln St.
Boston, MA 02111

The National Council for Homemaker-Home Health Aide Services, Inc.
67 Irving Place
New York, NY 10003

Check your local telephone directory under:
  Congregate dining
  Friendly visitor service
  Geriatric day care center
  Senior citizens' center
  Telephone reassurance
  Local office of the National Federation of the Blind

Grocery stores offer discounts to those over sixty-five in some cities, and will also deliver groceries one day per week to the housebound by volunteer.

Discounts for the elderly are common for museums, bus lines, adult education, and on meals at restaurants.

Dentists have outfitted mobile dental units in some localities and call at nursing homes to care for patients.

# NOTES

## CHAPTER 2

1. Olga Knopf, *Successful Aging: The Facts and Fallacies of Growing Old* (New York: Viking, 1975), pp. 189-90. Used by permission.
2. Edith M. Stern and Mabel Ross, *You and Your Aging Parents*, rev. ed. (New York: Harper & Row, 1965), p. 55. Used by permission.

## CHAPTER 4

1. Donna Swanson, "Minnie Remembers," *Face to Face* (May 1975), pp. 32-33. From *alive now!* Copyright by The Upper Room, used by permission of the author.
2. David A. Hubbard, "The Authority of the Bible," Fuller Theological Seminary *Bulletin Issue*, vol. 25, no. 2 (May-June 1975).

## CHAPTER 6

1. Gerhard E. Frost, *The Color of the Night* (Minneapolis: Augsburg, 1977), p. 112. Used by permission.

## CHAPTER 7

1. David O. Moberg, "Corban, Government Welfare and the Aged," *Eternity* (March 1967), p. 28.
2. Doris G. Jonas and David J. Jonas, *Young Till We Die* (New York: Coward, McCann & Geoghegan, 1973), p. 269.
3. Edith M. Stern and Mabel Ross, *You and Your Aging Parents*, rev. ed. (New York: Harper & Row, 1965), p. 187. Used by permission.

## CHAPTER 12

1. Bert K. Smith, *Aging in America* (Boston: Beacon, 1973), p. 211.

## CHAPTER 13

1. Etta Saloshin, quoted in "Retirement Is Just Beginning of Living for Countless Seniors," *St. Paul Pioneer Press*, Dec. 29, 1975.
2. Charlie W. Shedd, *Talk to Me* (New York: Doubleday, 1975), p. 15. Used by permission.

CHAPTER 15

1. Robert N. Butler, *Why Survive? Being Old in America* (New York: Harper & Row, 1975), p. 9. Used by permission.

CHAPTER 16

1. Bert K. Smith, *Aging in America* (Boston: Beacon, 1973), p. 29.
2. Henry Van Dyke, "A Friend in Need," in *The Blessings of Friendship* (Hallmark).
3. Henry Jacobsen, "Are We Ignoring the Elderly?" Reprinted by permission from July/August issue of *Moody Monthly,* copyright 1975, Moody Bible Institute, p. 28.

# BIBLIOGRAPHY

Bittner, Vernon J. *Make Your Illness Count: A Hospital Chaplain Shows How God's Healing Power Can Be Released in Your Life.* Minneapolis: Augsburg, 1976.

Brandt, Catharine. *You're Only Old Once.* Minneapolis: Augsburg, 1977.

Butler, Robert N. *Why Survive? Being Old in America.* New York: Harper & Row, 1975.

Cooley, Leland F. and Cooley, Lee M. *How to Avoid the Retirement Trap.* Los Angeles: Nash, 1972.

Donahue, Wilma T. and Tibbitts, Clark, eds. *The New Frontiers of Aging.* Ann Arbor, Mich.: U. of Michigan, 1957.

Frost, Gerhard E. *The Color of the Night.* Minneapolis: Augsburg, 1977.

Hyder, O. Quentin. *The Christian's Handbook of Psychiatry.* Old Tappan, N.J.: Revell, 1971.

Jackson, Edgar N. *The Christian Funeral: Its Meaning, Its Purpose, and Its Modern Practice.* New York: Channel, 1966.

Jonas, Doris G. and Jonas, David J. *Young Till We Die.* New York: Coward, McCann & Geoghegan, 1973.

Kelley, John T., ed. *Perspectives on Human Aging.* Minneapolis: Craftsman, 1976.

Knopf, Olga. *Successful Aging: The Facts & Fallacies of Growing Old.* New York: Viking, 1975.

Lewis, C. S. *The Problem of Pain.* New York: Macmillan, 1943.

May, Siegmund H. *The Crowning Years.* Philadelphia: Lippincott, 1968.

McMillen, S. I. *None of These Diseases.* Old Tappan, N.J.: Revell, 1967.

Metts, Wally. *The Brighter Side.* Chicago: Moody, 1977.

Nelson, James B. *Rediscovering the Person in Medical Care: Patient, Family, Physician, Nurse, Chaplain, Pastor.* Minneapolis: Augsburg, 1976.

Nouwen, Henri J. and Gaffney, Walter J. *Aging: The Fulfillment of Life.* Garden City, N.Y.: Doubleday, 1976.

Peterson, William J. *How to Be a Saint While Lying Flat on Your Back.* Grand Rapids, Mich.: Zondervan, 1974.

Poe, William D. *The Old Person in Your Home.* New York: Scribner's, 1969.

Puner, Morton. *To the Good Long Life: What We Know About Growing Old.* New York: Universe, 1974.

Simon, Anne W. *The New Years: A New Middle Age.* New York: Knopf, 1968.

Smith, Bert K. *Aging in America.* Boston: Beacon, 1973.

Smith, Elliott D. *Handbook of Aging.* New York: Barnes & Noble, 1972.

Stern, Edith M. and Ross, Mabel. *You and Your Aging Parents*. Rev. ed. New York: Harper & Row, 1965.

Tournier, Paul. *Learn to Grow Old.* New York: Harper & Row, 1972.

Reports

*No Longer Young, The Older Woman in America,* Work Group Reports from the 26th Annual Conference on Aging held in the Institute of Gerontology, The University of Michigan-Wayne State University, Ann Arbor, Mich. 48104. Copyright by The Institute of Gerontology, The University of Michigan-Wayne State University, 1974.

Pamphlets

"Checklist for Choosing a Nursing Home," Aetna Life and Casualty, 151 Farmington Ave., Hartford, CN 06115.

"Handle Yourself with Care" (tips on preventing accidents), U.S. Department of Health, Education, and Welfare, Washington, D.C. 20201, publication no. 805, 1969.

"How to Choose a Nursing Home, a Shopping and Rating Guide" (Prepared by Citizens for Better Care and the Institute of Gerontology, University of Michigan-Wayne State University, Ann Arbor, Mich. 48104, 1974, $1.).

Article

"New Outlook for the Aged," *Time* (June 2, 1975), pp. 44-51.

Moody Press, a ministry of the Moody Bible Institute, is designed for education, evangelization, and edification. If we may assist you in knowing more about Christ and the Christian life, please write us without obligation: Moody Press, c/o MLM, Chicago, Illinois 60610.